HOW TO
SETTLE AN ESTATE
OR
PREPARE YOUR WILL

HOW TO SETTLE AN ESTATE OR PREPARE YOUR WILL

TONI P. LESTER

A PERIGEE BOOK

To Melba and Conrad Lester

Perigee Books
are published by
The Putnam Publishing Group
200 Madison Avenue
New York, NY 10016

This book is designed to provide accurate information in regard to estates and estate planning. It is sold with the understanding that neither the author nor the publisher is engaged in rendering legal, accounting, or other professional services. Before settling an estate or preparing a will, the reader is encouraged to seek the services of a competent professional.

Library of Congress Cataloging-in-Publication Data

Lester, Toni P., date.
How to settle an estate or prepare your will / Toni P. Lester.
p. cm.
"A Perigee book."
ISBN 0-399-51444-9
1. Wills—United States—Popular works. 2. Executors and administrators—United States—Popular works. I. Title.
KF755.Z9L47 1987 87-35957 CIP
346.7305'6—dc 19
[347.30656]

Typeset by Fisher Composition, Inc.
Printed in the United States of America
1 2 3 4 5 6 7 8 9 10

Contents

Introduction

Before I discuss what you need to know about wills, let me tell you a story—one that turns into a nightmare. I hope you never have such an experience.

John and his wife were having marital problems.* For some time, they had had little to say to each other. In fact, at 40 years of age, John had decided that he wanted to start a new life for himself. His wife had her own job and was financially independent, so John was pretty sure that he would not have to pay her any alimony. He planned to move back in with his widowed mother, who was living on her husband's meager pension and monthly social security checks. John wanted to help take care of her. In addition to a joint savings account that he kept with his wife, John owned several pieces of real estate and stocks in the telecommunications business. His total net worth was about $300,000. He sometimes thought about drawing up a will. If he had ever gotten around to it he would probably have left some of his holdings to his mother and the rest to charity. But John was relatively young and apparently healthy, so he assumed that he would live longer than his mother and be around to take care of her himself. John thought he had plenty of time to settle his affairs. One morning while jogging, however, John suffered a heart attack and died within minutes. Because he died "intestate" (without a will) his estranged wife inherited everything. A few years later, his mother was forced to move into a state-run nursing home because his wife refused to give her any financial assistance.

Unfortunately, John's story is not unusual. Since a will shows what you and you alone want to see done with your money or property after you have died, it is important to have one. By not having one, John in effect said, "I will let the state I live in decide to give everything to my wife even though I am planning to divorce her."

These unfortunate stories are endless. Thus, an aunt's favorite nephew never gets to go to college because she neglects to draw up a will leaving him money in trust for school. The hostile parents of a deceased homosexual man leave his surviving partner with only the clothes on his

---

*The stories and characters portrayed in this book are fictitious. They were derived from real-life situations but are not intended to represent specific living persons.

back because the state they live in entitles an unmarried intestate's parents to inherit his property. A man's ungrateful son plans to sell to a private collector the priceless art collection that his father had planned to donate to a museum.

Yet despite the horror stories, many people still refuse or neglect to make wills. They come up with a host of reasons for not doing so. Perhaps you can recognize your excuses among the following:

"I know I should get one but I've been too busy lately to go see a lawyer."

"I don't really have very much so there's no point in paying an overpriced attorney for something that won't matter anyway."

"My family wants me to get a will, but I don't trust them. I know that once I get one, they'll be watching the clock until I die and they can get their hands on my money!"

"Even if I don't have a will, the law will make sure that the right people get it anyway."

It's true, the law will take care of it. But you should realize that the law has a mind of its own—one that may be in direct conflict with the way you think. Favorite friends and family members may be ignored while others get property and money you would never have wanted them to get. And it will probably also cost your family a great deal of time, money, and frustration to settle your estate without a will.

I hope you have now been convinced that it is important to have a will. However, if you are like most nonlawyers, you are probably overwhelmed and intimidated by the whole idea of preparing your own will or settling someone's estate without a will. Words like "probate" and "intestate" probably sound as foreign as Chinese! But don't worry.

In the chapters that follow you will become something of a "lay expert" on wills and estates, something that I'm sure you never imagined would happen. Of course, I recommend that you also consult a local attorney specializing in these subjects. But by familiarizing yourself with the relevant issues and with the words that attorneys use, you can save yourself time, confusion, and money, since lawyers usually charge for the time it takes to explain things to you.

In the first part of the book, I will explain in more detail what can happen to you if a loved one dies intestate, and what you will need to do to settle the estate. Obtaining death certificates, tracking down life insurance policies, making funeral arrangements, getting access to the deceased person's bank accounts, and dealing with tax considerations are some of the topics I will cover. The whole process of settling a person's estate has to be done whether or not there is a will. It's just that a will makes it easier for you to carry out many of these steps. And most important, with a will it is the deceased person's desires that are being carried out.

In the second part of the book I'll tell you how to go about preparing your own will. I will describe the different types of wills, talk about how you can get your own will prepared, and discuss how to pick an attorney and what types of fees you can expect. The rest of the book will be devoted to helping you decide what to leave and to whom to leave it, who you should ask to handle your affairs after you have died, setting up a trust, and what type of funeral arrangements you would like for yourself. I know these can be very difficult things to think about. But try to remember, if you don't do this now while you are calm and clear-headed, your family and loved ones will have to do it for you at the worst possible time, the time when they are in the midst of grieving over your loss.

At the back of the book you will find a simple glossary of the legal terms that are most often used by lawyers who handle wills, which will help you to avoid being intimidated by the fancy "legalese" that my profession often bandies about. Refer to the glossary if you come across a technical word that you don't understand.

Finally, throughout Part Two, Preparing Your Own Will, you will see samples of the language in wills that relates to some of the topics I'll be talking about. Two complete sample wills (one for a single person and one for a married person) can be found in the appendixes. If you're ambitious, you can use the sample language to make a first draft of your will. This way, when you do see your attorney, all he or she will have to do is review your draft and fine-tune it. As I have already said, I still strongly recommend that you seek the advice of an attorney before you settle an estate or make your will. Since the laws governing wills and estates vary from state to state, it would be impossible for me to cover all the details that might be unique to your state's laws. But wherever you live, I am sure that this book will make you a much more informed "wills and estates consumer."

ONE: SETTLING AN ESTATE WITHOUT A WILL

1

THE FUNERAL

Whatever your religious beliefs, the fact is that at some point the life that you know and experience today will end. Yet most of us are uncomfortable with the thought of death. We tell ourselves that death is something that happens to someone else, to people in the newspapers, to people who lead reckless lives, or to people much older than ourselves. Death is always something that will happen later in life; certainly not now.

This is a painful and emotionally charged topic, and it is not surprising that most people find it difficult to "prepare" for death by providing for their families and friends. The sad fact is that many of us do not make such preparations, leaving our loved ones the double burden of mourning our loss and of settling our estate without the guidance or benefit of a will. If you are someone who has been left in this unfortunate dilemma, you will have to rely on common sense, state law, and the advice of a good attorney to help you settle your loved one's estate. Perhaps hearing how Ann Jones handled a similar situation will also help.

Ann Jones, who is now 28, is the oldest of three children. Her parents were both in their fifties a few years ago. Her mother had been a legal secretary in a big law firm for almost 20 years. Her father was an unemployed steel foreman. The plant where he had worked for most of his adult life had been forced to close because it had been unable to compete with foreign and more technologically advanced competitors. Ann has two brothers. Bob, who was 17 at the time, was always getting into trouble with the law and had dropped out of school when he was 16. Her other brother, Stan, worked in a computer assembly plant for little more than minimum wage. He was 22. So Mrs. Jones was the real breadwinner in the family. Ann worked as a nursing assistant at a hospital in the neighboring town. A few years ago one Wednesday evening, Ann's mom was leaving work and was hit by a car as she crossed the street. She was pronounced dead when she reached the emergency room. Ann still recalls getting a phone call from her sobbing father giving her the terrible news.

When Ann arrived at her parents' house, she discovered that her father was so shocked and grief-stricken that he was sitting alone staring into space. Her brothers were bickering in the other room about whose fault it was that their mother had had to work so hard. As Mrs. Jones lay in the hospital morgue, no one seemed to be able to focus on what to do next. Since Ann was the oldest child, she automatically took charge. This had been her role in the family for as long as she could remember. Whenever there was a family problem, everyone always called on her for advice and help.

Mrs. Jones had never discussed with anyone what kind of funeral arrangements she would have wanted. Not very active in religious organizations, she sometimes attended Sunday services at the neighborhood Lutheran church, though she had been baptized a Methodist as a child. Since her mother had no strong ties to a church, Ann decided to arrange for her mother's funeral to take place at the local mortuary, Robinson's Funeral Home. Finding the phone number in the yellow pages, Ann called the home and was told that once they received her mother's death certificate, they could arrange to have the body brought to the home. So Ann went to the hospital, showed the receptionist the birth certificate saying that she was Mrs. Jones's daughter, and asked the receptionist to give her the death certificate. The receptionist gave Ann a death certificate that looked like the one on page 17.

Ann then went to the funeral home to talk to the funeral director about the type of funeral service that would be best for her mother. She convinced her dad to come with her. The funeral director showed Ann and her father a booklet filled with different types of caskets and a description of accompanying services. Together, the caskets and services were called funeral "packages," with some packages costing as little as $900 and some costing as much as $10,000.* Some packages included simple ceremonies performed by a minister in the funeral home chapel. Others included choirs and elaborate floral arrangements. Cremations were the least expensive.

It was very difficult for Ann and her father to face the fact that they were actually planning burial services for Mrs. Jones. That neither of them had much available cash only added to their sorrow. Ann especially felt guilty that she had to think of her mother's death in terms of dollars and cents. Painful as it was, Ann and her father picked a funeral package that included a simple ceremony, with the eulogy to be delivered by the funeral home chaplain. The cost was about $1,700. They decided that the

---

*Consult your local mortuary for exact prices.

Robinson's Funeral Home, Inc.

FUNERAL OF ...... Rosemary Jones .... ADDRESS ..... Anywhere, U.S.A. ....

Date of Death .... Place of Death ... General Hospital ....

MERCHANDISE, SERVICES and LIVERY	CASH ADVANCES FOR YOUR CONVENIENCE
Casket .... Deluxe .... $ ... 300	For Transcripts .. 15 at $4.00 ea. ...... $60.00 ....
Outer Receptacle	For Gratuities ....
Clothing or Burial Garments	For Crematory Charges ....
Memorial and/or Acknowledgement Cards .... $20.00 ..	For Cemetery Charges ....
For	For Bearers ....
Transfer of Remains to Funeral Chapel	For Clergy .... $200 ....
Embalming $400	For Organist .... $100 ....
Other Preparation of Remains	For Church Offering ....
Arrangement and Supervision	For Newspaper Notices ....
For	For Out of Town Funeral Director Charges ....
Hearse $200	For Out of Town Shipping Charges ....
Other Specified Funeral Coach	For ....
Flower Car @ $120	For ....
Limousing @ .. $100-per-limo (2 limos) .. $200	For ....
For	
Funeral Chapel $100	
Preparation or Operating Room	
TOTAL OF OUR CHARGES ...... $ ... $1,400 ...	TOTAL CASH ADVANCES .... $. 1,500 ......

TOTAL FUNERAL CONTRACT .... $ .. 1,700 ....

Date .... April 19 .... 19 . XX ......

The foregoing statement has been read by (to) me and I hereby acknowledge receipt of a copy of same and agree to pay the above funeral account and for such additional services and materials as are ordered by me, on or before

..... April 19 .... 19 . XX ...

The liability hereby assumed is in addition to the liability imposed by law upon the estate and others, and shall not constitute a release thereof.

NAME John Jones
Signature John Jones
Date 4/19/XX

Telephone ....

Funeral Director

body should be available for viewing the next day and that the funeral should take place that coming Saturday morning. The funeral home arranged to have the body buried in one of the town's cemeteries. Ann's dad had to sign the contract with the funeral home, which spelled out the prices and the services to be performed. The contract with the funeral home looked like the one on page 15.

Although they searched everywhere, Ann and her father were unable to find any copies of Mrs. Jones's life insurance policy. The funeral home would not agree to wait for them to find the policy. Since no one in the family had much money, Ann paid part of the bill with her charge card, and her father paid the rest of it with money from the joint checking account that he shared with his wife. They both hoped to find the policy and hear from the life insurance company by the time the charge card bill came a month later.

The visit to the funeral home was emotionally draining for Ann, so she asked her brother Stan to write a short obituary and have it printed in the morning paper. This way, she hoped to let her mother's friends in the area know about the funeral date. Many of her mother's friends, co-workers and relatives came to the funeral to offer their condolences. After the funeral, several family friends prepared a large meal for the funeral attendees at the Joneses' home. The last person didn't leave until late that evening. Ann, her father, and her two brothers were exhausted from the day's events. But in a way, the easiest part of Mrs. Jones's death was over for them. The most difficult part—getting used to her loss—was just beginning.

Using Ann's experiences as a starting point, let me take you through the steps you should take if you have to arrange for the funeral of a loved one.

DEATH CERTIFICATE

This is one of the most important documents you will have to obtain. You will need it to make funeral arrangements, to get life insurance proceeds, individual retirement account and pension distributions, and to make funeral arrangements. Normally, the decedent's attending physician will issue the certificate, and it must be certified by the department of health in your area. Try to get the death certificate as soon as possible. Also, get as many originals or notarized copies of it as possible, since most places you contact on behalf of the deceased person's estate will not accept photocopies. Sometimes funeral homes will arrange to get copies for you for a charge of about five to eight dollars per copy.

CITY OF **BUREAU OF VITAL RECORDS** **DEPARTMENT OF HEALTH**

Date ____________________

CERTIFICATE OF DEATH

Certificate No. 887-93-772-60

1. NAME OF DECEASED (Type or Print): Rosemary (First Name) ______ (Middle Name) Jones (Last Name)

MEDICAL CERTIFICATE OF DEATH *(To be filled in by the Physician)*

2 PLACE OF DEATH	a.	b. Name of hospital or institution, if not hospital, street address	c. If in hospital (check)	d. If inpatient, date of current admission
		Anywhere, U.S.A.	1 ☐ DOA 3 ☐ Outpatient 2 ☒ Emerg. Rm. ☒ Inpatient	Month / Day / Year

3a. DATE AND HOUR OF DEATH (Month)	(Day)	(Year)	3b. HOUR		4. SEX	5. APPROXIMATE AGE
April	18	19XX	8 PM	☒ AM	F	57

6. I HEREBY CERTIFY THAT: (Check One)

☒ I attended the deceased. ☐ A staff physician of this institution attended the deceased.

☐ Dr. ______________________ attended the deceased.

from April 1 19 XX to Same 19 ____ and last saw her alive at 10 AM

on ______________ 19 ____ I further certify that traumatic injury or poisoning DID NOT play any part in causing death and that death did not occur in any unusual manner and was due entirely to NATURAL CAUSES.

*See first instruction on reverse of certificate.

Witness my hand this [signature] ______________ D.O. / M.D.

Name of Physician Robert Smith (Type or Print) Address Anywhere, U.S.A.

PERSONAL PARTICULARS *(To be filled in by Funeral Director)*

7. USUAL RESIDENCE a. STATE	b. COUNTY	c. CITY TOWN OR LOCATION	d. STREET AND HOUSE NUMBER	e. INSIDE CITY LIMITS OF 7c
		Anywhere, U.S.A.		☒ YES ☐ NO

8. MARITAL STATUS (Check one)	9. CITIZEN OF WHAT COUNTRY	10. NAME OF SURVIVING SPOUSE (If wife, give maiden name)
1 ☐ Never Married 2 ☒ Married or Separated 3 ☐ Widowed 4 ☐ Divorced	U.S.A.	John Jones

11. DATE OF BIRTH OF DECEDENT (Month)	(Day)	(Year)	12. AGE AT LAST BIRTHDAY	If UNDER 1 Year mos.	days	If LESS than 1 DAY hrs.	min.
September	1	19XX	57				

13. USUAL OCCUPATION (Kind of work done during most of Year)	b. KIND OF BUSINESS	14. SOCIAL SECURITY NO.
Secretary	Legal	000-00-0000

15. BIRTHPLACE (State of Foreign Country)	16. OTHER NAME(S) BY WHICH DECEDENT WAS KNOWN
New York	N/A

17. NAME OF FATHER OF DECEDENT	18. MAIDEN NAME OF MOTHER OF DECEDENT
William Smith	Owens

19a. NAME OF INFORMANT	b. RELATIONSHIP TO DECEASED	c. ADDRESS (City) (State)
John Jones	Husband	Anywhere, U.S.A.

20a. NAME OF CEMETERY OR CREMATORY	b. LOCATION (City, Town, State and Country)	c. DATE OF BURIAL OR CREMATION
Lutheran Cemetery	Anywhere, U.S.A.	April 22, 19XX

21a. FUNERAL DIRECTOR	b. ADDRESS
Robinson Funeral Home	Anywhere, U.S.A.

BUREAU OF VITAL RECORDS **DEPARTMENT OF HEALTH** **THE CITY OF**

This is to certify that the foregoing is a true copy of a record in my custody.

CITY REGISTRAR

The Department of Health does not certify to the truth of the statements made thereon, as no inquiry as to the facts has been provided by law.

DO NOT ACCEPT THIS TRANSCRIPT UNLESS THE RAISED SEAL OF THE DEPARTMENT OF HEALTH IS AFFIXED THEREON. REPRODUCTION OR ALTERATIONS ARE PROHIBITED BY LAW.

FUNERAL ARRANGEMENTS AND FUNERAL HOMES

One of the most painful tasks, making the funeral arrangements, must be taken care of immediately. Many religions require that a deceased person be buried within a certain period of time. Family and friends have to be notified, and the details of the burial have to be thought through. As Ann's story shows, if the deceased person has never told you how he or she wanted the funeral arranged and there is no will providing such information, planning the funeral can be especially hard. Although Ann had no problems with Robinson's Funeral Home, many people are not so lucky. Like any good consumer, she should have done some detective work first. Checking with the minister of the local Lutheran church or with friends with similar experiences would have been a good start. But Ann was carrying a heavy burden of sadness and responsibility. This is when many of us are most vulnerable to making mistakes and being taken advantage of.

Unfortunately, in the past some dishonest funeral home operators *did* take advantage, and gave a bad name to the entire industry. They charged exorbitant fees and negligently misprepared bodies. In response to public criticism of questionable funeral industry practices, in April of 1984 the United States Federal Trade Commission (FTC) adopted rules governing the disclosure by funeral homes of the specific charges for their services. The rules are still in effect and provide that funeral homes must tell you over the telephone what they charge for certain services. This enables you to do some comparative shopping without having to visit each individual home.

The rules also state that if you do visit a funeral home, the home must give you a list of general prices without any obligation on your part to use that home. The list must cover specific costs for individual services to be provided. It must also spell out if cash in advance will be required for certain purchases that the funeral home may make on your behalf, like ordering flowers, sending obituary notices, or paying members of the clergy. The invoice from Robinson's Funeral Home complied with these guidelines.

The Federal Trade Commission rules also state that a funeral home must tell you that it cannot charge you for embalming the body without your authorization, except in certain special circumstances. Contrary to popular belief, restoring the body to look lifelike, or "embalming" it, is not required by law in many states. Homes also cannot require you to choose more expensive burials over cremation. And they must inform you that cremations do not have to take place in caskets.

If you have, or if the decedent had, limited resources, and there is no strong religious need to bury the body in a casket, you may want to choose cremation as a respectable and inexpensive alternative to burial. Cremations are usually less expensive. Smaller containers called "urns" are often used instead of caskets to house the decedent's remains. These urns will often cost less than caskets.

Competently run funeral homes can be a great help in times of trouble. Sometimes funeral homes will agree to wait to be paid from the proceeds of a life insurance policy. (How you can get those proceeds will be discussed in the next chapter.) For those who are not affiliated with a particular church or religious group, funeral homes often can provide several helpful services. They can hold religious services, arrange to get death certificates for you, send obituaries to the newspapers, and perform their traditional role of handling the burial or cremation. Of course these services cost money, and in some instances it may be cheaper for you to do some of the miscellaneous tasks yourself. So remember to ask for the itemized statement of prices that is required by the FTC rules to make sure that you are not being overcharged.

There are several organizations you may wish to consult for advice on finding a funeral home or to make a complaint about one that you have dealt with.

Conference of Funeral Service Examining Boards
520 E. Van Trees Street
P.O. Box 497
Washington, IN 47501
Phone: (812) 254-7887

National Funeral Director's Association
135 West Wells Street, Suite 600
Milwaukee, WI 53203
Phone: (414) 276-2500

Jewish Funeral Directors of America, Inc.
122 East 42nd Street
New York, NY 10168
Phone: (212) 370-0024

And, of course, you can always write to the FTC to voice a complaint:

U.S. Federal Trade Commission
Funeral Industry Rule Division
Washington, DC 20580

OBITUARIES

One of the most touching things that a family or friend can do for a deceased loved one is to write the obituary. Obituaries serve two important functions: They can be a public testament of your admiration and love for the deceased. In a more practical vein, obituaries can give the date and place of the funeral or memorial service, since it is impossible to notify everyone that might be concerned. They also sometimes describe the cause of death, the kind of life the person led, the extent of his or her community involvement and charitable activities, and how much he or she was loved. Most major newspapers charge about ten dollars per line for a ten-line obituary. Lengthier obituaries are usually printed only as newsworthy items at the discretion of the editor.

Now we have covered making funeral arrangements. Ann's next chore was to help her father get the proceeds of her mother's life insurance policy, and to arrange for the distribution of any other property or income that her mother's family or friends were entitled to under the law.

2

SETTLING THE ESTATE WITHOUT A WILL

Ann avoided talking to her father about the family's financial situation until after the funeral. It's hard enough for anyone to talk about money problems, and harder still when the problems come as a result of a loved one's death. As I have already mentioned, Mr. Jones had been unemployed for some time and Ann's brothers contributed little to the family's upkeep. Ann helped out when she could, but her income was really just enough to support herself. Her father had all but depleted the money in the joint checking account to pay the funeral costs and general housekeeping expenses. But bills still had to be paid, and food had to be bought.

While she was alive, Mrs. Jones always handled the family's business affairs. It was she who paid all the bills with her and her husband's paychecks. After her mother died, Ann looked everywhere for the files and personal papers that she was sure her mother had kept. It wasn't until a week after the funeral that Ann found a cardboard box full of Mrs. Jones's personal papers under her parents' bed while she was cleaning up. In the box were Mrs. Jones's life insurance policy certificate, the deed to the house, bank and retirement account papers, pension information, title to the family car, and other important papers. After looking through the papers and the rest of the house, Ann was able to make the following list of Mrs. Jones's belongings at the time of her death:

- A savings account in Mrs. Jones's name in the amount of $10,000 at Merchant's Bank.
- A joint checking account in the names of both Mr. and Mrs. Jones at

Merchant's Bank, naming the surviving spouse as the exclusive account owner.
- An individual retirement account (IRA) Certificate from Merchant's Bank naming Ann as the beneficiary.
- A life insurance policy from Mutual Life Insurance Company in the amount of $50,000, naming Ann as the beneficiary (the certificate looked something like the one on page 23).
- Title to the four-year-old Ford Escort that Mrs. Jones had bought after her employer had given her a raise, probably worth about $3,000.
- A deed to the Joneses' three-bedroom Cape Cod, naming Mr. and Mrs. Jones as cotenants with the right of survivorship. (Ann knew that the mortgage on the house was paid and that the house was valued, at the time of her mother's death, at about $100,000.)
- The sterling silverware that Mrs. Jones had gotten as a wedding gift, which Ann valued at $3,000.
- Diamond earrings that had been given to Mrs. Jones by her grandmother, which Ann valued at $500.

Ann also called her mother's employer that day and was told that Mrs. Jones was covered by a pension plan, which enabled her father to receive a small monthly check once they received a certified copy of Mrs. Jones's death certificate.

Ann was not surprised to learn that her mother had named her as the beneficiary on the life insurance policy and the individual retirement account. Ann's father had never really handled money matters very well. Her mother probably felt that Mr. Jones's interests could best be served if Ann managed the money. Ann was also not surprised to see that her mother had named neither of her two brothers as beneficiaries, since her mother had always felt that they could not be counted on to support the family. Ann knew that her father and brothers would probably bitterly resent her mother's favoritism, especially since it would directly affect everyone's financial situation.

Since there was a pressing need for cash to pay for food and utility bills, Ann called the life insurance company and Merchant's Bank to see if she could get the insurance proceeds and the money from Mrs. Jones's savings account. The insurance company representative told Ann that the company would send her the $50,000 about two weeks after she sent them a certified copy of the death certificate and a notarized letter from her stating that she was the beneficiary of the policy. However, the clerk at the bank informed her that since the bank account was in her mother's name, Ann would not be able to obtain access to it without a certified copy of the local court's order giving Ann authority to administer Mrs. Jones's estate. The clerk did tell Ann, however, that because Ann was the named beneficiary, Ann could have the funds in the individual retirement

Anywhere Life Insurance Company—Insurance Certificate

Insured: Rosemary Jones — Sex: Female Age: 45
Certificate Number: 000-0000
Plan: Lump Sum Life Insurance
Insured Amount: $50,000
Certificate Issue Date: January 5, 1976
Named Beneficiary: Ann Jones — Relationship: Daughter
Annual Premium (Payable Quarterly): $400

Plan Benefits: The Insured Amount is payable to the beneficiary at the death of the Insured upon receipt of proof of the death of the Insured, if the Insured dies while this insurance policy is in force. A detailed description of plan terms and conditions is attached hereto and is a part of this agreement.

Ten-Day Right to Return Certificate: You have ten days after you receive this Certificate to examine it. Within those ten days you can return the Certificate to the Company for any reason. If you do so, the insurance evidenced by this certificate will be canceled. Any premium paid will then be refunded and the insurance evidenced by this certificate will be void from the beginning.

This certificate has been signed on the Issue Date by the Company at its home office, 22 Main Street, Anywhere, U.S.A.

President: ______ Secretary: ______

There are many types of life insurance policies. Some are sophisticated investment tools for their purchasers. Others simply help a person to see to it that his or her funeral arrangements are paid for. This policy certificate allowed Mrs. Jones to have one lump sum amount distributed to her daughter at the time of her death. The premium (the cost of the policy) increased as Mrs. Jones became older. Attached to the certificate was a detailed description of the terms of the policy. Among other things, the policy provided that only premiums would be refunded if the insured had not paid premiums when due. Also only premiums paid would be refunded to the beneficiary if the insured committed suicide within two years from the date of the original certificate.

account once Ann gave the bank a certified copy of her mother's death certificate. The account contained about $5,000.

Ann was intimidated by the idea of going to court. Like many people, she thought of the court system as a long series of bureaucratic mazes designed to make average people feel stupid. So, on the advice of a friend, she got the name of a local estate attorney and called to make an appointment to discuss what she should do next. The next day, Ann and her father visited the lawyer. Ann brought with her the list she had made of her mother's assets. After the lawyer reviewed the list, she confirmed what Ann and her father had recently learned—that some of Mrs.

Jones's assets, like the IRA and the life insurance proceeds, could be distributed to Ann relatively quickly and simply. Since the checking account was a joint account with a "right of survivorship" provision, the account technically became the property of Mr. Jones at the time of his wife's death. This was also the case for the house, whose deed gave each spouse the right of survivorship. The rest of the property, the attorney continued, like the savings account, the car, and the silverware and earrings, had to go through a bureaucratic court process before any of it could be distributed to the family.

The attorney explained that the process involved petitioning a special local court called a "probate court"* to allow a decedent's assets to be distributed according to his or her will. If there was no will, the estate would be distributed under the intestacy laws of the state where the decedent was domiciled.* The attorney said the term "intestacy" was simply a legal term that meant "dying without a will." In Mrs. Jones's case, since she died intestate, her husband was entitled to receive only one-third of court-controlled assets. The remaining two-thirds could be divided equally among Ann and her two brothers.

Mr. Jones became visibly upset when he heard the lawyer say he could get only one-third of his wife's assets. The attorney explained that in some states the husband might have been able to get a greater percentage, but this wasn't the case in Mrs. Jones's home state. The attorney then explained that before anyone in the family could get anything, all of Mrs. Jones's debts would have to be paid out of the funds from the estate, including attorneys' fees and any money owed to state and federal taxing authorities. Then and only then could the family divide what was left.

The attorney recommended that Ann ask the court to allow her to be the administratrix of the estate. This involved getting a court order designating Ann as the administratrix, taking possession of all estate property, and preparing a formal inventory of assets owned and debts owed by Mrs. Jones. Ann would also have to get a court-authorized appraiser to value the estate, file for and pay all state and federal taxes, and notify and repay all of Mrs. Jones's creditors. After getting appointed, Ann could then have the attorney handle all the details. Of course, no significant steps could be taken by the attorney without Ann's consent. The attorney said that the whole process would take a little over a year before Ann and her family could get the remaining assets they were entitled to.

The lawyer finished by saying that her legal fees would be about two to three percent of the value of the estate. This was based on the recommended table of fees payable to estate attorneys established by state law. Since the attorney would be doing virtually all of the work, she expected

---

*See glossary for definitions.

Ann to pay her the entire fee. The attorney did agree to wait until the estate was settled before she was paid her fee. She did, however, require that all court costs and filing fees be paid as they were incurred.

Mrs. Jones had been a fairly frugal person. After her husband lost his job, she worked a great deal of overtime to try to make ends meet. Fortunately, she had been able to save some money and had even opened an IRA. She only owed about $1,000 in charge card debts at the time of her death, and the house had been paid for years before, since the Joneses had gotten a fifteen-year mortgage when they bought it. Despite the absence of extensive debts, state law required that Mrs. Jones's estate's administrator print a notice in the local papers telling all creditors with an interest in Mrs. Jones's estate to file their claims within six months. The notice looked something like the one on page 26. As you can see from the notice, creditors usually have up to six months from the date of the notice to file a claim against an estate.

The charge card company, Mrs. Jones's only creditor, filed a claim against the estate for $1,000 three weeks after it saw the attorney's notice in the paper. At the court's instruction, the attorney paid the company. But the family still had to wait the entire six months before it could have access to the rest of the savings account or Mrs. Jones's other personal possessions.

During the year that it took for Ann to settle her mother's estate, the family had several arguments about how the balance of the estate should be distributed. Ann invested the $55,000 that she received from the life insurance company and the IRA in mutual funds. Although she was generous with the money that she gave her father out of the dividends that she earned, her father resented the fact that he had to ask her for money. Mr. Jones was a very proud man, and it had embarrassed him deeply to have to rely on his wife for financial support. Looking to Ann for the same type of help after his wife's death only made him feel more insecure. He believed that he should have had exclusive use of the money his wife left to Ann.

But Ann disagreed. She knew that her mother had been constantly worried about how her husband mismanaged his financial affairs. Because he squandered money, at the time of his layoff he had no savings and was forced to let his wife support him. It was then that Mrs. Jones began to save a little money each year and to open the IRA for herself. She had never told her husband what she was doing.

The court appraised the value of Mrs. Jones's court-controlled or "probate" assets at approximately $15,500, after subtracting the charge card debt. Mr. Jones felt that he alone should be entitled to these assets as well, but Ann's two brothers had other ideas. They knew that Ann would take care of their father, and they planned to take their two-thirds sibling's share without giving anything back to him. In fact, they wanted to sell the silverware, the jewelry, and the car and divide the proceeds

Legal Notice

Commonwealth of Anywhere
The Probate and Family Court

Docket No. 112 2599

Estate of Rosemary Jones, late of Anywhere. In the county of Anywhere.

NOTICE

A petition has been presented in the above-captioned matter praying that the estate of Rosemary Jones, in the county of Anywhere, be distributed to all legal heirs.

If you are a creditor having a claim on the estate and desire to file a petition to be paid said claim, you or your attorney must file a written appearance in said Court at Anywhere within 180 days of the date of this notice.

In addition you must file a written statement describing the nature and amount of your claim and including copies of all pertinent documentation evidencing the obligation of the decedent to pay such claim within 180 days of the date of this notice.

Witness, John Doe, Esquire, First Justice of said court at Anywhere, this first day of ______ in the year of Our Lord one thousand nine hundred and eighty ____.

______________________Register of Probate

among themselves. Ann felt that her brothers were being extremely selfish. She knew that her mother would have wanted those personal possessions to stay in the family. But when the law leaves intestate property to be shared equally, as was the case in the state where Mrs. Jones died, all beneficiaries must agree about how they will share the use of that property. If they cannot agree, any one beneficiary can decide to sell the property and the others will not be able to prevent the sale. They will, however, be able to take their share of the proceeds of the sale.

So when the time came, Ann's brothers were able to get what they wanted.The car and the silverware were sold. Ann's father got to keep $5,165, his one-third share of his estate. Ann and her brothers each got $3,445, their one-third interest in the remaining two-thirds of the estate. Fortunately, because of the small amount involved, Mrs. Jones's estate was exempt from federal and state estate taxation. Even so, the family was never quite the same after that. There were bitter feelings on all sides about how things had been handled. Nevertheless, Mrs. Jones's estate was finally "settled."

Using Ann's case as an example, let us examine the types of things that you should remember when you have to settle someone's estate without a will.

INVENTORY ASSETS

As soon as you can, make a complete list of the deceased person's assets. The inventory can be used for tax filing and probate court appraisal purposes. As was the case with Ann, making an inventory can sometimes be made difficult if you have trouble locating the decedent's files and important papers. Some people keep such papers in bank safe deposit boxes, for which only they have a key. In such a case, the only way for you to obtain access to the box is to have the certified court statement naming you as the administrator of the decedent's estate. Checking with local banks to determine which bank has the decedent's deposit box may also prove difficult until you get the court authorization. List all probatable items under the heading "Probate Assets" and all nonprobatable items under the heading "Nonprobate Assets."

PROBATE AND NONPROBATE ASSETS

When compiling your list, determine which assets you can have distributed without going to probate court. This is important because the probate process can take a long time and family and friends may need the use of some of the assets, especially money, much sooner. Also, the beneficiaries of nonprobate assets can usually get them without your help, so you will have more time to focus on the items that do require a court process. Ann was able to figure out which assets were not subject to probate on her own.

Assets with named beneficiaries or assets which are owned jointly with survivorship rights are usually not subject to probate. Life insurance proceeds, joint bank accounts, house deeds with rights of survivorship, and stocks or retirement accounts with named beneficiaries fall into this category. Jointly held property will probably have to have title transferred to the survivor. This can be done through a title company or with the help of an attorney. Banks can reopen joint accounts in the survivor's name. For all of these things, you will usually need to produce a certified copy of the death certificate and some authentication of the beneficiary's signature.

In some states banks have a policy of freezing all joint accounts until the survivor can submit a copy of an inheritance tax waiver. The waiver is given in some states when it can be established that no taxes are due. In Mr. Jones's case, a requirement like this at Merchant's Bank would have caused him great financial burden. Even though there were no state or federal taxes assessed against his wife's estate, he would have had to wait for the taxing forms to be filed and the taxing authorities to send him a waiver. If you are in this situation, some estate attorneys advise that you immediately withdraw funds from the joint account before the bank finds out about the death, then set up a new account at another bank in your name. Since the legality of such a step is questionable, I would strongly urge you to consult a local attorney first.

CHOOSING AN ADMINISTRATOR

If a person dies intestate, the court will appoint an administrator to settle the estate. Often this person is a family member or a close business associate. Normally, someone will volunteer, and the court will appoint whomever it considers the best person for the job, as was true in Ann's case. The court will give the administrator a certificate or "letter of administration" (if there is a will this is called a "letter testamentary"), which states that the administrator has authority to settle the estate. This is a valuable piece of paper, since it enables the administrator to withdraw funds from the deceased person's bank accounts, receive stock dividends, and generally do whatever must be done to take possession of estate assets.

After the administrator has the estate appraised, he or she should file the appropriate federal and state tax returns as soon as possible. (See Chapter 3 for details.) Once all taxes and claims have been paid, the administrator can petition the court to be allowed to distribute estate assets to the decedent's heirs. Although the general rule is that the heirs get what's left of the estate only when all other claims have been settled, sometimes probate courts will allow an administrator to give the decedent's family a hardship allowance to cover necessary living expenses during lengthy probate proceeding.

Sometimes the decedent may have a business that must either be sold or be kept operating. The administrator is responsible for doing this too. However, the administrator can hire a professional business manager to operate or wind up the business on his or her behalf. If you do need to hire a manager, make sure you to have an experienced attorney draw up a professional services contract for you and the manager to sign. Among other things, the contract should stipulate that no major decisions or actions affecting the business can be taken without your written consent.

CHOOSING AN ATTORNEY

It will also probably be necessary for you to hire an attorney to help you settle the estate. Although, theoretically, you can do this yourself, the probate process, with all of its notification and procedural requirements, is often very time-consuming and complicated. Since an estate attorney will know the local probate requirements, you can save yourself the hassle of keeping abreast of all of these things yourself.

Attorneys are usually paid out of the probatable estate. Many states establish what percentage of the estate is payable to the attorney. If you think this amount is too high, try to negotiate an acceptable fee with your attorney. Sometimes the lawyer will accept an hourly rate, which may result in lower fees. Whatever you agree to, make sure you have discussed fees and are satisfied with the fee arrangement before signing any contracts to retain the attorney as your representative. The fees charged by Ann's attorney were within the range of what her lawyers in her state charged. (Choosing an attorney will be discussed at greater length in Part Two.)

FAMILY SQUABBLES

Disagreements like that within Ann's family are not unusual. When a person dies without a will leaving specific instructions on how to distribute and handle their assets, someone is bound to suffer. In this case, Mr. Jones probably felt that he suffered the most. Understandably, he felt he was entitled to much more than he received. We will never know whether Mrs. Jones named Ann as a beneficiary for convenience sake or because she did not want her husband to have any of her assets. It is likely, however, that she would have been heartbroken to hear that her sons had forced their father to sell her jewelry, car, and silverware. For some unfortunate reason, some of us can be most selfish when faced with someone else's misfortune. You can avoid such family feuds if you have a will prepared.

Of course, beneficiaries of an estate can agree to distribute property differently from what is required by state intestacy laws, and the court will probably approve the distribution. An agreement of this type is called a "settlement by compromise."

SINGLE VERSUS MARRIED

In some states property acquired by either spouse during the marriage is considered "community property" and as such is legally shared by both spouses on a 50-50 basis. In these states a surviving spouse is allowed to keep his or her 50-percent interest in that property when the deceased spouse dies intestate. Community-property states also often allow the surviving spouse to keep one-half of any property acquired by the deceased spouse either before the marriage or during the marriage where title is in the deceased person's name only ("separate property"). The children get to divide the remaining property among themselves. There are many other ways in which estates of married people can be distributed without a will (see the terms "dower" and "curtesy" in the glossary), but the most important thing to remember is that state laws vary, so you should definitely seek the advice of a local attorney.

The steps for settling the estate of an unmarried person without a will are basically the same. Assets not subject to probate can be given to named beneficiaries relatively quickly, and assets subject to probate must go through the same notification and petition process. The main difference involves how state laws distribute the assets after creditors, attorneys, and the taxing authorities are paid.

In Mrs. Jones's case, if she had been single with no children, her state's intestacy laws would have given the balance of her estate to her parents. If her parents were dead, her brothers and sisters would have divided everything among themselves equally. Without any descendants or legal heirs, Mrs. Jones's entire estate would have "escheated" or gone to the state's coffers. State law therefore generally looks to the next nearest relative when it comes to distributing intestate property. This can be a real problem for people who are estranged from their relatives or who would prefer to have their assets go to friends or other unrelated loved ones. Unless you make a will, these friends may get little of what you leave behind.

If you are a single person who is committed to a relationship, but for some reason the two of you do not marry, take heed. Some states may consider long-term heterosexual relationship as "common law marriages" and allow the surviving common law spouse to inherit the partner's estate in accordance with state intestacy laws. Other states may not. Even so, where there are no children, real or common law spouses may have to share a substantial part of the estate with their spouse's parents, siblings, cousins, or even more distant relatives in some cases! This is true whether or not the deceased spouse knew or even liked these relatives. Your need for financial assistance has no bearing on how the state will distribute the estate. If you find yourself in financial straits, you will have to rely on the good graces of your partner's relatives.

Nontraditional partnerships, like long-term homosexual relationships, are not recognized as common law marriages in the vast majority of states. Thus, the surviving partner of a homosexual relationship may have no property rights at all. This is especially true in situations in which parents and relatives either do not know about the relationship or disapprove of it. Partners in this type of relationship may find themselves watching as parents or even more distant relatives remove all of the decedent's personal belongings and property, leaving nothing for them. Of course, having a will prepared can prevent this from happening. Whatever type of relationship you are in, I'm sure you can see that the best way to make sure your loved ones get the gifts you intend to give is to have a will prepared.

3

TAX CONSIDERATIONS

The area of estate and gift taxation is a complicated one. Volumes have been written that deal only with this topic. There are accountants and tax experts who specialize in this area alone. While I cannot go into all the details of estate and gift taxation, I can tell you about some of the issues that you should be aware of if you are settling someone's estate.

Like many people, you may think that there will be little left for the heirs of the estate you are settling once the federal government gets through assessing taxes. There are countless stories of the estates of wealthy people that were taxed at as much as 50 percent. That, combined with equally exorbitant state inheritance taxes, often does leave very little. But don't worry. If the estate you are settling is relatively moderate in value, you will probably not have to pay any federal taxes at all! And many states allow you to exempt up to a certain amount of your inheritance from state taxation as well.

Of course the administrator of an estate is usually responsible for paying all taxes associated with the death *before* any other distributions can be made. This includes any income or other taxes that were owed by the decedent, as well as the tax on any income that the estate earned during probate. The most important death taxes that you should be familiar with, however, are federal estate taxes, state inheritance taxes, and state and federal gift taxes.

FEDERAL ESTATE TAXES

The federal government imposes a tax on the right of the decedent to *transfer* his or her estate to heirs at death. Normally, the administrator or executor of the estate, as the case may be, is responsible for filing the lengthy return (see Appendix A, IRS Form 706) and paying the tax *before* any of the estate is distributed. This must take place no later than nine months after the date of death, and severe penalties will be levied unless an extension is granted. Also, if the tax is not paid by the administrator, the amount that each beneficiary receives will still be subject to the tax later.

Unless you have a sizable estate to settle, however, you don't have to worry about paying federal taxes, because the IRS exempts certain amounts from taxation. The exempted amount is $600,000. Federal estate taxes on amounts over the exempted amount range from as low as 18 percent to as high as 55 percent. Because the value of Mrs. Jones's estate was less than the exempted amount in the year she died, her estate did not have to pay any federal taxes.

After allowable deductions, credits, and exemptions, the entire "gross estate" of the decedent is taxable. Generally, this includes all "willable" property interests owned at death. (For a discussion of what's willable, see Chapter 7.) Contrary to what you might think, the value of many nonprobate assets must be added to the gross estate. This includes life insurance policies with named beneficiaries (unless the insured transferred complete ownership of the insurance policy to the beneficiary), the full value of jointly held property, and any debts or royalties due the decedent.

Federal taxes are then imposed on the gross estate *minus* certain allowable deductions, some of which are *adminstrative expenses,* like attorney's and administrator's fees; *miscellaneous expenses,* like court costs and appraiser's fees; *funeral expenses; claims against the estate,* like debts due to creditors; *charitable gifts* made by the estate; *casualty* or *theft losses* on estate property awaiting probate that is not covered by insurance; *unpaid mortgages* on estate property; and the *marital deduction.*

Except for the marital deduction, these deductions are relatively self-explanatory. The marital deduction is extremely important to surviving spouses. Subject to certain requirements that the surviving spouse evidence control of the property, the marital deduction enables the survivor to deduct from the gross estate the value of that part of the estate which passes to the spouse because of a will, intestacy law, a life insurance policy, or a joint tenancy with the right of survivorship. Thus, the marital deduction can substantially reduce a sizable estate for tax purposes. For instance, had Mrs. Jones's estate been larger, Ann could have deducted $100,000, the value of her parents' house, from her mother's gross estate. This would have reduced any federal estate taxes due because Mr. Jones became exclusive owner of the house, since the deed named him as a co-owner with a right of survivorship. Thus, the administrator would have been entitled to claim the $100,000 as a marital deduction on behalf of the estate, and the taxable estate would have been smaller.

After deductions are taken from the gross estate, the IRS will give you credits against any taxes due. These credits include any gift taxes or state estate or inheritance taxes actually paid. Please remember that federal tax law can change from year to year, so it is important to contact the IRS or consult a tax attorney before preparing your estate tax returns.

STATE INHERITANCE TAXES

Some states follow the federal government and impose estate taxes on the deceased person's estate. Many states also levy an inheritance tax on the heirs or beneficiaries of the estate. The latter is usually a percentage of the actual amount received or the value of property received. Close relatives of the deceased often pay a lesser percentage, with the rates gradually increasing for more distant relatives and unrelated beneficiaries. As is the case with federal taxes, certain portions of inherited property are exempt from state taxes. Unfortunately, distant relatives and non-relatives are sometimes granted smaller exemptions than close relatives. Some state inheritance taxes exempt life insurance proceeds received by named beneficiaries from inheritance and estate taxation. Others do not.

GIFT TAXES

I am sure you must be thinking, "Do you mean to tell me that the estate will *also* have to pay gift taxes?" The answer is yes, maybe. You probably didn't realize that the IRS imposes a tax on givers of gifts. Fortunately, moderately propertied people will probably not have to pay any gift taxes. With certain exceptions, you can give up to $10,000 to any one person every year without having to report the gift or pay any tax. There is no limit on the number of people that you can give this amount to, as long as each person gets only $10,000. In fact, you don't even have to report these gifts to the IRS. But when you start giving gifts valued at more than $10,000, you will have to report those gifts to the IRS. You will also have to pay taxes after the aggregate of those gifts becomes greater than $600,000. At that time you will be subject to the same rates that apply for federal estate taxes. Any gift taxes paid will be deductible for the purposes of federal estate taxes, and gifts made to charities and to spouses are not subject to gift taxes at all.

Before the early 1980s, the federal gift tax on a given amount was significantly smaller than the estate tax on the same amount. As a result, many people gave gifts to their loved ones *before* they died to avoid having their estate taxed at the higher rate. As you can imagine, the IRS didn't look too kindly on gifts given for the specific purpose of avoiding estate taxes, so it adopted a guideline providing that the IRS would consider a gift to be given to avoid estate taxes if it was given within three years of the decedent's death. A gift given within this period was thus included by the IRS in the gross estate for tax purposes. Many states also followed this three-year death rule.

Today the IRS no longer has such a rule. Since gifts and estates are now taxed at the same rate, there is no longer a presumption that people will give gifts to avoid estate taxes. Thus, any gifts given during the decedent's lifetime will not be included in the gross estate for tax purposes.

You should keep in mind, however, that some state taxing authorities still apply the three-year death rule, and will expect you to include in the gross estate any gifts given by the decedent within the past three years. It will be up to you as the administrator to prove that the gifts were not given for the purpose of avoiding the tax. If you can do this to the satisfaction of the taxing authorities, you can save the estate a great deal in state taxes. Be sure to consult a local attorney to find out about state taxes in your area.

CHECKLIST FOR SETTLING AN ESTATE WITHOUT A WILL

Here are a few things that you should remember to take care of during the first few weeks and months after a loved one dies:

First and Second Days after Date of Death*

- Notify family members, friends, and employers by phone.
- Get death certificate from the hospital.
- Locate life insurance policy.
- Visit funeral home to make funeral arrangements.
- Phone in, or have funeral home phone in, the obituary notice to the local newspaper.

First Week after Date of Death

- Hold funeral services.

---

*All dates are approximate.

Second and Third Weeks after Date of Death

- Find and organize decedent's important papers (such as title to property, life insurance policies, and pension information).
- Make an inventory of assets, listing assets and dividing them into categories labeled "Probate" and "Nonprobate."
- Start obtaining possession of all nonprobatable assets, such as jointly held bank accounts and life insurance policies. If you are not a named beneficiary of these assets yourself, inform the beneficiaries and give them the necessary documentation.
- Make an appointment to see an attorney to discuss probate procedures.

Second to Ninth Month after Date of Death

- Continue efforts to obtain possession of nonprobatable assets.
- Have attorney commence probate proceedings on your behalf, get court-appointed appraiser to value probate assets, notify creditors of their right to make claim to probate assets, hire any business managers needed.
- Have attorney file appropriate tax forms on your behalf.

One Year after Date of Death

- Distribute remaining probate property to heirs and beneficiaries according to state intestacy laws.

PART TWO: PREPARING YOUR OWN WILL

4

TYPES OF WILLS AND GENERAL REQUIREMENTS

You may be thinking, "I thought there was only one type of will." Not so. States recognize many types of wills, provided that certain requirements are followed to make them enforceable.

PROPER WILLS

When it comes to making sure that your estate is adequately protected from state intestancy laws, there *is* only one type of will as far as I'm concerned. For argument's sake I will call it a "proper will." A proper will is neatly typed, has all the necessary devices and bequests required by state law (to be discussed in the next few chapters), is signed by you and at least three disinterested witnesses of at least eighteen years old or older, has its pages numbered, has been reviewed by a competent attorney and is filed with the proper authorities. I will tell you how to have a will like this prepared in the next few chapters.

ORAL OR NUNCUPATIVE WILLS

As I'm sure you have guessed, an oral will is one in which the testator tells someone how to dispose of his or her property after he or she dies.

Because there is a strong potential for the person who witnessed the oral will to lie to his or her benefit about what was actually said or the testator's intentions, oral wills are generally not enforceable. However, some states do recognize "nuncupative wills" or oral wills made in front of witnesses during the testator's last illness. People who use nuncupative wills are typically soldiers and sailors in active military service and terminally ill or deathbed patients. Many state will acknowledge such wills only if the value of the property bequeathed is less than some nominal amount like $1,000, and if the property is personal property, such as money or jewelry, as opposed to real estate. Often there must be at least two witnesses and the testator must die within a short period after the will was made.

HANDWRITTEN OR HOLOGRAPHIC WILLS

Slightly higher on the will totem pole are holographic or handwritten wills. These wills are valid in many states if they are handwritten, dated, and signed by the testator. Some states also require that holographic wills be signed by one or more disinterested witnesses (that is, witnesses who will not benefit in any way from the will).

I strongly caution you not to use a handwritten will if you can avoid it, since there is always the risk that the will will be declared unenforceable. (I'm sure that you remember all the tabloid stories about the host of "authentic wills" written by the late millionaire Howard Hughes.) It sometimes takes a great deal of time and money for prospective beneficiaries to prove that the will they hold is the real one. Usually the testator's handwriting must be verified, and if there is any doubt about the signature, a disgruntled relative or friend can challenge the will during probate on the grounds that the will is a forgery.

The only time when it may be advisable for you to prepare a handwritten will is in an emergency, if you are afraid that you will not be able to have a better one prepared in time. This is better than dying without any will. In such a case, prepare the will, sign and date it, and get at least three disinterested witnesses to sign it if you can. To prevent accusations that someone altered the will, make sure that no words are crossed out or erased on the will itself. As soon as the emergency is over, however, go to your attorney and have a proper will drawn up.

POOR MAN'S WILL

Technically, documents creating nonprobate assets, like insurance policies with named beneficiaries, joint tenancies on real estate, and joint bank accounts with the right of survivorship, are not wills since they do not have to be submitted to the probate court for enforcement. In fact, people will often purposely acquire such jointly held accounts, stocks, and real estate in order to avoid having this property subjected to lengthy probate proceedings. Normally, the documentation for such property is a standard form drawn up by the issuing bank, underwriter, or broker. No attorney's fees are charged. That is why they are called "poor man's wills." Since the documents clearly show that the holder intended to own the property in the described manner, states will not require that the property be distributed according to their intestacy laws. Also, the only way to change the nature of the ownership is to revise the ownership document. A phrase in a will stating that the same property must be distributed in a different manner is not enforceable, since the words in the will conflict with the ownership document. Thus, a phrase in a will in which Mrs. Jones named her husband as the only beneficiary on her life insurance policy would not have replaced Ann as the beneficiary unless the policy itself had been previously revised by Mrs. Jones to replace Ann's name with Mr. Jones's name.

LIVING WILLS

"Living wills" are also not wills in the technical sense, since they do not state how the testator wants property to be disposed of at his or her death. They instead describe how the testator wants to be treated if he or she becomes incapacitated in some way, such as being in a permanent coma in a hospital. In this document, the testator usually directs family and friends to authorize a physician to terminate life support systems under these circumstances. This in effect allows the testator to die naturally. If you think that you would like to leave such instructions, I would advise you to have a living will prepared at the same time that you have your will prepared and to keep both documents in the same place.

WHO CAN PREPARE A WILL

Anyone with "capacity" can make a will. In other words, you must be mentally competent and of the age required by your state's law. Eighteen is the typical age for capacity. The word "capacity" has a harsh ring to it, but don't worry. You don't have to have a high IQ or be a saint to make a will. You must merely be able to understand that what you are preparing is a will and that your property will be disposed of accordingly after you die. You can be a convicted felon or as eccentric or vindictive as you want.

You can leave all your money to the circus and disinherit all of your family.* Such an action will not necessarily be taken to mean that you are crazy as long as it can later be shown that you realized that it is customary for people to leave something to their families and decided to go against tradition. Or you can be like the woman in a recent news story who directed in her will that her entire mansion, complete with priceless antiques and works of art, be demolished. Despite objections from art curators, her wishes were carried out by her executor, since it was proven that she was perfectly sane when she prepared her will.

You cannot, however, be forced or coerced into making your will. A will written in response to a threat to harm you or your friends, or to sue you, would be unenforceable. Sometimes wills can be challenged on the grounds that the testator did not have the capacity to make the will. It is the responsibility of the challenger to prove this, through the use of witnesses, psychiatrists, and other appropriate people. Witnesses may be asked to recall if the testator behaved irrationally or appeared to be under the influence of drugs or alcohol, since all of this can show that the decedent did not have capacity when the will was drafted. To avoid the risk of this happening to your will, try to prepare it when you are in a calm frame of mind, under the guidance of a good attorney. Finally, make sure that the will is signed by disinterested witnesses. Such a will will thwart most capacity challenges.

*One is, however, prohibited in many states from completely disinheriting a spouse.

5

NAMING AN EXECUTOR

As you've already learned from Part One, the executor is the person or company who manages your estate while it goes through the probate process. When there is no will, this person is called an administrator. The executor must pay all taxes and creditors, and finally dispose of the estate's assets according to the requirements of the will. Most states have a table of allowable fees that must be paid to the executor for these services. Like attorney's fees, they are usually a percentage of the value of the estate.

Probate can often take a long time, and there is a chance that estate assets will be damaged or stolen, or will depreciate in value while the estate is in probate. Once the court appoints the executor, it is his or her job to take possesion of the assets and settle the estate in the most effective and efficient manner possible. If there is a business involved, the executor must exercise prudent judgment and either continue operations or sell it. If estate money is lost or property is damaged as a result of the negligence or ineptness of the executor, he or she may be liable to the estate's beneficiaries for damages. Also, if through his or her own negligence the executor distributes the estate before paying the necessary taxes, he or she may be personally responsible for paying the taxes. Some states may even require that the executor post a bond to cover these contingent liabilities before he or she can begin her duties.

As you can see, this is a very big responsibility and shouldn't be handed over to someone lightly. Perhaps you are thinking of choosing your mother or your best friend to do this for you. They are trustworthy and reliable. But they may not have the necessary expertise to run your business or handle a sizable estate. So if you have substantial investments or have your own business, you may instead want to pick a reliable trust company or the attorney who drafts your will to be your executor. Since these people are in the business of handling estates, they can probably represent your beneficiaries' interests more effectively.

Typically, however, what happens is that people name either spouses or friends to be their executors. Most people probably feel more comfortable knowing that a loved one, rather than a business entity, will be taking care of their interests. These are the people we feel we can trust the most. But the named executor usually ends up hiring an experienced attorney or a trust company, so the result is the same. The only difference is that the attorney or trust company will expect to share a substantial portion of the executor's fees. That's what happened to Ann Jones.

Also, keep in mind that whoever you pick may not feel comfortable as or qualified to be your executor, so make sure that you discuss this beforehand with the person you choose. Finally, give him or her a copy of your will or, if you don't want its contents known, give your executor a letter telling him or her how to find your will in a place that will be conspicuous after your death. However, I would recommend that you tell your executor at least the general terms of your will. That way the executor will be better prepared to carry out your desires when the time comes. It is also very important for you to tell your executor *where* to find your important papers after you have died. If you don't feel that you can trust the executor with this information, then you have probably chosen the wrong person.

A typical provision in a will naming a spouse or friend as an executor might read like this

> I hereby appoint ______, who resides at ______, to be my executor. I direct that my executor pay all my just debts, taxes, and funeral expenses and make my funeral arrangements in the manner set forth in this my last will and testament. If ______ does not survive me, then I appoint my friend ______ to be my executor.

6

THE GORY DETAILS

None of us like to think about what will happen to our bodies after we are dead. Thoughts like, "How should I be buried?" or "Maybe I should donate my organs to a local hospital" remind us that we are mortal. The thought that our bodies and minds will no longer exist one day is almost too much for many people to bear. If your religion offers you the solace of a soulful afterlife, the distastefulness of this topic may be softened. But even so, something has to be done with your body after you die, and the best person to decide what that will be is you.

ORGAN DONATIONS

As I'm sure you know, every day someone dies because a doctor is not able to find an organ needed for a critical transplant operation. You may want to put a provision in your will that tells your doctor or the attending physician of an emergency room (should you be in an accident) to use your organs to help save someone else's life after you have died. Some may find this type of bequest a little barbaric, but to the recipient, it can mean a second chance for life. A typical organ donation will provision would read like this:

> I hereby direct that immediately after I have been certified dead by a competent physician, my heart, liver, and eyes will be removed surgically by the appropriate medical personnel and used for the specific purpose of prolonging the life of someone who otherwise would die without the necessary organ transplant.

FUNERAL ARRANGEMENTS

I have already told you in Part One a good deal about funeral prices and how an administrator makes your funeral arrangements when there is no will. But who better to make these arrangements than yourself? Why not visit several funeral homes and ask them about the prices and services that they offer? Your will can state how much money should be spent on the funeral, whether you should be buried or cremated, and what kind of service you would like. No one can go against your wishes. It is your executor's responsibility to make sure that your plans are carried out. Think of how much easier it would have been for Ann Jones and her father if her mother had done this.

Here's a standard provision covering funeral arrangements:

> I direct my executor to have my body cremated at ______ funeral home located at ______ in ______. I have already discussed the type of service I want with the director of the home and have filled out an invoice for the desired service and the type of urn that I want my ashes to be placed in. A copy of the invoice can be found in my safe deposit box at ______ bank located at ______ in ______. I direct that my funeral expense be paid out of my estate and that I be buried at ______ cemetery, located at ______ in ______, and that a suitable marker be erected at my grave.

LIVING WILLS

In Chapter 4 I told you about the living will. This is a document that you should have prepared and kept with your will and other important papers. It directs your physician to discontinue using artificial life support systems should you become permanently incapacitated. It is not, however, a part of your will, since it covers what should be done to you while you are still alive. A simple living will would probably read like this:

> I, ______, wish to tell my family, loved ones, and physician that I cannot bear the thought that I would be kept alive indefinitely if for some reason I became physically incapacitated to such an extent that my brain no longer functioned or that I was in a permanent coma. I therefore direct that, if any of the above events occur, there be no technological life support systems used to keep me alive and that I be allowed to die in this dignified way according to my wishes.

I should caution you that living wills may not be enforceable in some states. Thus families and hospitals may institute court proccedings to go against your wishes and require that you be kept alive with life support systems. However, if you feel strongly about this, go ahead and have one prepared anyway, since there is always the chance that the law will change before anything happens to you.

7

WHAT'S WILLABLE AND WHOM TO WILL IT TO

Not long after Mrs. Jones died, Ann's father died of a heart attack. Under the state intestacy laws, Ann and her brothers were left the house. They decided to sell it and split the proceeds. It was also at that time that Ann decided to quit her job and go to college to get a degree in business and hospital administration. Several years later she had a new career as a manager in a hospital comptroller's office. The job paid very well and Ann was soon able to save and invest more and buy some property with a friend.

Ann never forgot the problems that her family experienced because her mother had died without a will. Ann knew that the state intestacy laws would give her two brothers all of her assets when she died. Although she loved them both, there were other things that she wanted to have done with her property. So sometime last year she decided to have a will prepared.

Ann did a preliminary draft of the will herself and then took it to a lawyer to review. Here is a list of her assets at that time:

- A brand-new Honda Prelude.
- A certificate of deposit for $25,000.
- A savings account in the amount of $3,000.
- A life insurance policy naming her boyfriend, George, as the beneficiary.
- A one-half interest with George in a summer beach house.
- Designer clothes and jewelry.
- Furniture.
- A high-quality stereo system.

Ann also owed $3,000 in charge card debts.

You can leave almost anything you want to in a will, as long as you have a recognizable property interest in what you leave. This includes anything that you alone have title to, like Ann's car. It also includes your percentage share of any jointly held property, like Ann's interest in the summer house. If Ann decided to leave personal property like her clothes, it would be called a "bequest." If she decided to leave real estate like the beach house, it would be called a "devise." To make it easier for you to remember, I will call both things "gifts."

LIST OF YOUR BENEFICIARIES, ASSETS, AND LIABILITIES

The first thing Ann did was to make a list of the people she wanted to name as beneficiaries. At the top of the page she wrote down all her vital statistics, including birth date and social security number, as well as the names of her nearest relatives and close friends. Included on the list were her brothers, Bob and Stan, and her boyfriend, George. Since Ann had always had pets and loved animals she also included the local animal protection society on the list. You can put anyone you wish to on the list. Typical lists included spouses, parents, brothers and sisters, close relatives, friends, religious organizations, and charities.

Then, to help her decide what to give, Ann made a list inventorying what she owned. Assets were listed under column headings that described whether the assets were personal property or real estate (see the glossary for definitions of personal property and real estate). These categories were important, because her state's estate laws treated these two types of property differently when it came to distributing them under the will. There will be a further discussion of how the law treats real and personal property left in a will later in this chapter.

Ann also tried whenever possible to identify her assets with serial numbers or specific descriptions. This would later help the executor locate all items named in the will. Finally, she gave an estimate of the net value of each asset. This would help the executor determine the value of the estate for tax purposes. (See the glossary for a definition of net value.)

Ann also made a list of all of her debts, including charge card debts and her share of the loan she owed on a house she co-owned with her boyfriend. Since Ann knew that her creditors had to be paid before her beneficiaries, the lists gave her a good idea of what would actually be left to give after her creditors were paid. (The form that Ann used to prepare her list of assets, liabilities, and potential beneficiaries can be found in Appendix B.)

GIFTS OF PERSONAL PROPERTY

It was then time for Ann to think about how and to whom she wanted to give her personal property. Cash, family heirlooms, musical instruments, jewelry, your car, and books are all types of personal property. You can either give all of your personal property to someone, give specific pieces of property to different individuals, or have your executor sell everything and divide the proceeds according to your wishes. Ann wanted to leave money to her brother Bob and her stereo system to her other brother, Stan. Using some standard will language, Ann drafted the following statement to put into her will:

> I give and bequeath the sum of $3,000 to my brother Bob if he survives me.
>
> I give and bequeath to my brother Stan my Technics stereo receiver, turntable, and speakers (serial numbers ______), if he survives me.

But when her lawyer reviewed her draft he informed her that her state's law allowed specifically named gifts to take priority over cash gifts. In other words, even if there was not enough money in the estate to pay cash gifts, Stan would still get the stereo system. However, if there was no stereo system after she died, Stan's gift would be "adeemed" or lost. On the other hand, Bob's cash gift would have to be paid out of the general estate assets, and if the estate had no cash, nonspecific gifts would have to be sold to pay him.

Finally, the lawyer explained that all cash gifts would be "abated" or reduced proportionately if there was not enough money to pay all the donees. Thus, if Ann were to leave $5,000 to Bob and $5,000 to a charity, but at the time of her death there was only $2,000 left in the estate, Bob and the charity would only get $1,000 each. There was one way to partially solve this dilemma, however. Ann could state in her will that she wanted some donees to get their cash gifts *before* other donees. Following his advice, Ann asked the lawyer to revise her draft to say:

> I hereby direct that, if there is not enough cash to pay all cash bequests, my executor should first pay my brother, Robert, his cash bequest before any other cash donees are paid.

Now if there is only $2,000 left, Robert will get all of it and the charity will get nothing.

CONDITIONAL GIFTS

You can also attach conditions to gifts that you leave. For instance, you could decide to leave money to a college on the condition that the money be used to give scholarships to students from your home state. However, there are some conditions that you *cannot* place on gifts left in your will. You cannot put restrictions on certain kinds of behavior. For example, you shouldn't leave a family heirloom to your cousin on the condition that she divorce her husband and marry someone else, or change her religion.

There are also other conditions that you cannot will. You cannot require that a beneficiary of a gift do something illegal as a condition of receiving his or her gift. For instance, a will stating that "June Williams must kill my hated enemy, Judge Smith, before she can receive the $700,000 bequest" will clearly not be carried out.

The risk you run when you leave a legally unacceptable conditional gift is that the entire gift will be voided by the probate court and your intended recipients will get nothing.

Ann decided to leave a conditional cash gift of $4,000 to the animal protection society, which read as follows:

> I give and bequeath the sum of $4,000 to X Animal Protection Society, located at 1 Elm Street in the City of Anywhere, U.S.A. Said sum shall be used by the society for the specific purpose of seeing to it that abandoned dogs are placed in new homes.

Since it is often difficult for institutions to carry out this type of restrictive bequest, her lawyer suggested that she add the following sentence to her provision:

> If for some reason the Society cannot fulfill the condition I have attached to this bequest because of impracticality, the Society can use the money for whatever purpose it deems appropriate so long as it is used for the prevention of cruelty to animals.

As you can see, the whole area of leaving conditional gifts by will is a complicated one that requires your consultation with a good attorney.

MARRIED VERSUS SINGLE

As I have explained in previous chapters, you can give away anything in your will that you have a recognizable property interest in. When you are single, unless you have entered into a co-ownership arrangement with someone else, you alone have interest in the property you own. Whether it is a car or a house, all your property is yours alone to will. But when you are married, this is often not the case.

Many states have community property laws stating that a spouse has a "community" or one-half interest in any property acquired during the marriage. This includes everything except "separate property" or those things bought by a spouse that he or she alone has title to or that the spouse received by gift or from a will. If you live in a community property state, you can only will *your share* of the community property, and the beneficiary in effect becomes a joint owner with your spouse.

Since Ann isn't married, she is free to leave most of her property to whomever she pleases. However, she can leave only her *one-half* interest in the beach house to someone, since she owns it together with George.

CHANGING YOUR WILL: THE CODICIL

You should always keep your will up to date, changing it as your life changes in ways that affect what you want your will to cover. You may make new friends or have children, or your financial situation may change. You can change your will as many times as you want to reflect these events. But be careful. You should never cross out words or write additional words on your will, since someone could later contest it on the grounds that it was tampered with.

If you wish to completely change all the terms of your will, you should have a new will drawn up, which states at the beginning:

> This is my last will and testament, and I revoke all wills and codicils previously prepared by me.

If you want to change only certain parts of your will, you need to prepare what is called a "codicil." The codicil should refer to the previous will and be signed and witnessed in the same way as a will. For instance, if Ann Jones later decided that she wanted to leave her brother Bob her one-half interest in her beach house, she would have to have a codicil prepared. (A sample codicil appears in Appendix E.)

8
TRUSTS

You may remember that Ann's brother Bob was leading a very irresponsible life when his mother died. He dropped out of high school and did little or nothing to contribute to the financial welfare of his family. During the years after his parents' death, he wandered from job to job, never gaining any real financial security. It was not unusual for Bob to "borrow" money from Ann or from his brother, Stan, and never pay them back. Although he often promised them that he would go back to school and handle his life more responsibly, it was clear to everyone that Bob would never change.

Although Ann frequently became annoyed with Bob, she still loved him and worried about how he would fare if anything should happen to her or Stan. She wanted to leave Bob something in her will but was afraid that he would squander it immediately. Her mother had probably felt the same way about leaving anything to her unemployed father.

Ann was not sure what to do so she asked her attorney for advice. He suggested that she leave Bob a monthly allowance, the principal of which would be held in trust by a trust company. Usually a trust is set up when a trustee (like a bank trust department or some other business entity) is named in a will to manage a certain amount of money by investing the principal. The will then directs that the interest earned, some of the principal, or both should be paid to a named beneficiary. Often the trustee is instructed to pay a monthly allowance over a specified period of time (after which all trust money is paid to the beneficiary) or until the trust funds are depleted.

Like the executor, the trustee is extremely important. The trustee has what is called a special or "fiduciary" relationship with the person who creates the trust (Ann, in this case) and the trust beneficiary (Bob). The trustee must manage the trust according to the trust creator's wishes and *never* use trust funds for his or her own benefit. Any violation of this fiduciary relationship will result in serious legal penalties.

After interviewing several trust companies and on the advice of her attorney, Ann chose the trust department at Merchant's Bank to manage the trust that she would leave for Bob. She also decided that a monthly allowance of $200 would be paid to Bob for the rest of his life. If there was any money left over after that, Ann wanted it to go to the animal protection society.

The language drafted by her lawyer to cover the trust in Ann's will looked like this:

> I hereby direct my executor to have the trust department of Merchant's Bank, located at ______ in Anywhere, U.S.A., set up a trust in the amount of $______, which shall be the trust estate to be held for the benefit of my brother, Robert Jones. Said trustee shall have the following rights and responsibilities:
>
> 1. Unless it contravenes state or federal law, to invest the trust estate in personal property, stocks, bonds, securities, real estate, and any other kind of property or investment that any other trust company using prudent business discretion and knowledge would use.
> 2. The earnings on the principal of the trust shall be used to pay to my brother, Robert, a monthly allowance of $200, to be paid to him for the rest of his life, after which the balance of the trust shall be paid to the animal protection society referred to elsewhere in this will.

Please keep in mind that trust companies charge for their services. Usually the fee will be a monthly or annual percentage of the value of the trust. This will reduce the value of the trust money available to be paid to the beneficiary.

The above trust language is only being used to familiarize you with the issues that are involved with creating a simple trust in a will. But as is the case with estate and inheritance taxes, the topic of trusts is governed by a separate body of law, and it would be wise to consult your attorney before deciding to provide for one in your will.

9

CHOOSING AN ATTORNEY

After you have spent some time thinking about what you want your will to cover, you may want to prepare the first draft yourself. Feel free to use some of the language I have used in these chapters, as well as any of the appropriate provisions in the appendix. After you've made your draft, however, you should have it reviewed and put into its final form by an attorney.

The attorney should be licensed to practice law in your state, and preferably live there. Although it is not absolutely necessary for the attorney to have years and years of experience, you will want to make sure that he or she is fully aware of all the relevant issues. A good place to start when you are trying to find an attorney is to ask your friends or business associates. Advice from people who have recently experienced the death of a loved one and can tell you whether the will that was prepared for the decedent held up in probate court without any problems will be especially helpful.

If you can't find an attorney through friends or relatives, call your local bar association and ask for the names of several wills and estates attorneys in your area. Another good place to look is in a book called the *Martindale and Hubbel Law Directory*. This book lists almost all the practicing lawyers in the country by firm or company and state, gives their addresses and phone numbers, educational background, and area of expertise. You can find it in your local public library. If you have time (and I advise you to take it), telephone a few. Here are some important questions that you should ask:

- Where did they get their education and relevant experience? (A lawyer who has worked only on corporate mergers for the past several years and never on wills is not someone you would want to pick!)

- Do they charge you for the first hour of consultation? (Some lawyers will not charge for the first hour as a demonstration of good faith. This way you can visit them and if you are not satisfied you can go elsewhere without having to pay anything.)

Keep in mind that, except for the discount legal clinics that you see advertised on television, most lawyers charge by the hour for their services. Small firms or solo practitioners should charge between $75 and $150 an hour. Law firms can charge as much as $150 to $250 an hour! Although the legal clinics I referred to advertise that they charge a flat fee (about $100) for preparing wills, be careful. The flat fee is based on preparing a very simple will—usually one that involves a single bequest or devise and has no complicated trust arrangements or bequests.

Whomever you choose as your lawyer, make sure that you agree with that person in writing about what the fees will be. If you are worried that the fees are too high, try to negotiate a "cap" or limit on how high the fees can go. While the cap can protect you from ridiculously high fees, I should caution you that once the lawyer reaches the limit, he or she will not do any more work until you have agreed to pay more. If you don't reach an agreement, you can choose to go elsewhere.

Once you and your lawyer have put your will into its final form, it would probably be a good idea for you to give either a copy or the original to your lawyer. Also, let your family and friends know who your lawyer is. This way, if anything happens to you, they'll know to check with your lawyer to find out where your will is. Knowing who your lawyer is will also be helpful to your executor, since he or she may want to use that lawyer to probate your will.

CHECKLIST FOR PREPARING YOUR OWN WILL

The following is a general checklist of steps you will need to take when you decide to have your own will prepared:

- *List potential beneficiaries.* Make a list of all the people you would like to leave something to. This might include relatives, friends, companies, charities.
- *Pick an executor.* This is someone (either a person or a business entity) whom you trust to see to it that the terms of your will are carried out.
- *List all your assets and liabilities.* Remember to give an estimate of the net value of your assets.
- *Designate which assets for which beneficiaries.* Make a list of alternative beneficiaries in case these beneficiaries are not alive when you die.

- *List special gifts.* If you think you will want to place conditions on certain gifts or to establish a trust for a beneficiary after you die, list these gifts in a separate category so that you can have your attorney draft this language for you.
- *Prepare first draft of will.* Using sample will language, prepare a first draft and compile a list of questions that you will need to ask your attorney.
- *Choose an attorney.* Hire an attorney to review your draft will and to draft any special will language that is necessary.
- *Put your will in a safe place.* Also make sure that you tell both your executor and your attorney how to find your will.

10

TEN IMPORTANT QUESTIONS ABOUT WILLS AND ESTATES

Here are some questions that people often ask when they have to settle an estate without a will or want to have their own will prepared:

What does the term "probate a will" mean? This is the judicial process by which a will is proved to be authentic, an administrator or executor is appointed, the decedent's creditors and taxes are paid, and the beneficiaries under the will receive the gifts left to them. If there is no will, all estate property (property owned by the decedent at death) will be distributed according to state law.

How long does the probate process take? It can take anywhere from a year to a few years, depending, among other things, on how much property the decedent left, where the property is located, and whether the will is challenged.

How much will it cost me to have a will prepared? A simple will in which you leave everything to one person, or only a few simple gifts to friends or family members, should probably only cost you between $100 and $300. The exact cost will depend on how much initial drafting you are willing to do yourself and what fees your lawyer will charge. Since most lawyers charge by the hour (from as low as $75 to as high as $250 an hour!), a more complex will providing for such things as conditional gifts or the establishment of trusts will probably cost you more. Make sure that you get your lawyer to give you an estimate of what he or she thinks it will cost. If your lawyer says that he or she cannot give you an estimate, look for another lawyer.

Will my creditors be able to force my family to pay my unpaid debts when I die? No. The executor (if you leave a will) or the administrator (if you don't leave a will) of your estate will see to it that your debts are paid after you die. The executor or administrator will use the property that *you own* when you die (estate property) to pay your creditors. All beneficiaries under your will receive only what you want to leave them *after* all estate taxes and debts are paid. However, estate property usually does not include many types of life insurance policies, pension benefits left to a spouse, or jointly owned property owned under an agreement that gives the survivor exclusive ownership upon the death of one of the co-owners. So your creditors will not be entitled to any of this property. Many states also exempt family homes from the claims of creditors.

Can I disinherit my wife or my uncle in my will? Generally, you can specifically disinherit anyone you like, but in most states *you cannot completely disinherit a spouse.* Most states require that the surviving spouse receive at least a certain percentage of the value of the deceased spouse's property.

I'm single and I live with my boyfriend. Who will inherit my property if I die without a will? Exactly who gets what will depend on the law of the state in which you live. Generally, if you are married your spouse is allowed to inherit a large portion of your estate property. If you are not married, most states allow your closest surviving family members to get your property when you die. If you have been living together long enough, some states may consider you and your boyfriend to be "common law spouses" and let your boyfriend inherit a substantial portion of your property. Many states will not. To protect yourself from the uncertainties of this situation, have a will prepared.

I am gay and my family does not approve of my lifestyle. If I prepare a will leaving everything to my partner, can my parents later successfully have the will overturned? No. As long as you have "capacity" you can leave whatever you want to whomever you want. Generally all this means is that you must be of legal age at the time you are having your will prepared (in most states this is 18) and that you must understand the nature and consequences of the will document that you are preparing. If you fear that your family may challenge your will after you die, have an attorney help you prepare the will to ensure that local capacity requirements are being properly met.

Why can't I just leave a simple note in writing saying who I want my property to go to? In most instances it is not advisable to leave a handwritten will, since there is always the chance that it will be challenged as a forgery. Some states do recognize handwritten wills written by deathbed patients or soldiers in combat, but even these states usually require that there be witnesses.

How can I see to it that the money I leave my young niece is not squandered by her? You can direct in your will that an adult guardian manage the money on behalf of your niece until she is of legal age, after which she gets everything. As an alternative, you could direct that a trust company invest the money for your niece and pay her interest or dividends until she comes of age.

When should I rewrite my will? In many ways your will is like a snapshot of where you are in terms of relationships, income, and property at a certain point in your life. So if there are any substantial changes in any of these things, you should seriously consider changing your will. For instance, you may want to change beneficiaries, include your new spouse in your will, or pick a new executor if the one you chose dies or becomes unavailable. Make sure, however, to *have a whole new will prepared, one that explicitly revokes all previous wills prepared by you.* Never alter or write over portions of a will, since this will give your will the appearance if having been tampered with.

Glossary

This glossary contains important legal terms that can help you understand the law of wills and estates.

Abatement. The process of determining under state law how to pay off general gifts left in a will when there are not enough estate assets to pay for them. Many states will simply decide to decrease the size of all general gifts proportionately.

Ademption. Sometimes an item of personal property left as a gift in a will is no longer in existence. When this happens, the intended recipient receives nothing. This unfortunate occurrence is called ademption.

Administrator. When a person dies intestate (without leaving a will), the administrator is the person whom the probate court (or its equivalent) appoints to settle the decedent's estate (Administratrix is the feminine form of the word.)

Assets. All a person's property and possessions. When used in the context of wills and estates, the term refers to all property of the deceased person that is used to pay all claims against the decedent's estate.

Bequest. A gift of personal property by will. The act of giving such a gift is called "bequeathing."

Codicil. A document that changes some portion of an original will. To be enforceable, the codicil usually has to meet the same technical standards as the original will with respect to capacity, witnesses, and so forth. Usually, if the will is invalid for some reason, so is the codicil. (See Appendix E for a sample codicil.)

Common Law Marriage. The cohabitation of a man and a woman in such a way that it appears to be a legal marriage. Some states will treat common law marriages in the same way as legal marriages for the purposes of divorce settlements and estate distributions.

Community Property. Generally, property acquired by either spouse during a marriage that many states consider jointly owned property for divorce and estate distribution purposes. The property is considered jointly owned whether or not only one of the spouses contributed financially to the marriage. A spouse can usually give away by will only one-half of any community property. (See also "separate property.")

Curtesy. A widower's legal right to receive a certain portion of his wife's real estate for life. The curtesy right is usually given to widowers when their wives die intestate. (See also "dower.")

Decedent. A person who has died.

Devise. A gift of real estate given by will.

Domicile. The place that you plan to permanently make your home, which is usually where you pay your taxes, vote, and have a mailing address. This is to be contrasted with a "residence," which is a place in which you plan to stay only temporarily—even for a few years. Many states have enacted the Uniform Execution of Foreign Wills Act, which says that the law of the state where your domicile is located will generally determine whether or not your will is valid and enforceable.

Dower. A widow's legal right to receive a certain portion of her husband's real estate during her lifetime. Dower is usually given to widows when their husbands die intestate. (See also "curtesy.")

Embalming. Preparing a body for burial by preventing it from decaying.

Escheat. The taking of estate property by the state when there are no other beneficiaries to receive it.

Estate. The assets and liabilities left by a person who has died.

Executor. The person or company named in a will to settle the decedent's estate. (Executrix is the feminine form of this word.)

Holographic Will. A will written totally in the handwriting of the testator.

Homestead Laws. State laws that protect widows and widowers from having their houses repossessed and sold when there aren't enough other assets in their deceased spouse's estate to pay off estate debts.

Intestacy Laws. State laws governing how estate property is to be distributed when the decedent dies without a will.

Intestate. Having died without leaving a will; also, a person who dies without leaving a will.

Letters of Administration. Document given to the administrator of an estate authorizing him or her to settle the estate. The document enables the administrator to take possession of all estate assets.

Letter Testamentary. This is the same as a letter of administration except that it is given to the executor of an estate.

Liabilities. All of a person's debts and obligations. When used in the context of wills and estates, it means all the debts and obligations that are a part of a deceased person's estate.

Net Value. The value of that part of property you own *minus* the value of any encumbrances or restrictions on that property. Encumbrances include mortgages on your house or liens from a finance company on your car. For example, Robin financed the $100,000 purchase price of her house last year with a mortgage loan from her bank. As of today, she has paid $3,000 on the mortgage, leaving $97,000 still owed to the bank. At the same time, the house's market value has also increased to $150,000. Thus, $53,000 ($150,000 minus $97,000) is the equity or net value of Robin's house today. It is that net value (which may increase as the house appreciates in value and her mortgage obligation decreases over time) that is Robin's to leave in a will.

Personal Property. Any property that is not real estate.

Probate. The legal process for proving that a will is valid and enforceable. For the purposes of this book, however, the term "probate" is also used to refer to the legal and court process by which estate assets are distributed in a stipulated order of priority to will beneficiaries, intestacy beneficiaries (if there is no will), creditors, taxing authorities, and executors and administrators.

Probate Assets. Estate assets that can only be distributed to the will's designated beneficiaries after the estate goes through the probate process.

Probate Court. The court that has jurisdiction to authorize the distribution of estate property according to either state intestacy laws or state laws governing will distribution.

Probate Laws. State laws governing how estate assets are distributed pursuant to wills.

Real Estate. Land and things attached to the land; for example, houses and trees.

Residuary Estate. All estate property that is left over after a will's gifts have been distributed and debts and taxes have been paid.

Right of Survivorship. The right of a joint property owner to own jointly held property completely if the other joint owner dies. Usually the title or deed to the property will say "John and Jane Doe, as joint owners with the right of survivorship."

Separate Property. Anything that is not community property. Usually, property acquired by one spouse before marriage or inherited during the marriage is owned exclusively by that spouse.

Settling an Estate. The act of disposing of a deceased person's assets and liabilities according to state and federal law.

Testator. A person who makes a will.

Trustee. A person or business entity who has legal title to certain property but holds it for someone else's benefit. A trustee can be named in a will, or can be named by the probate court if the will calls for a trust to be created but fails to name a trustee.

APPENDIXES

Appendix A. IRS Form 706—United States Estate Tax Return Form

Form 706 is the form that the executor of an estate must submit to the Internal Revenue Service to determine if federal estate taxes are due. The IRS also publishes an instruction booklet on how to fill out the form. You can call 1-800-424-FORM and ask the IRS to mail you the form.

First Section of Form 706. As you can see, both the top part of the first page and the "General Information" section on page two of Form 706 simply ask for vital statistical information about the decedent and the executor. You will also need to know the decedent's domicile. This is the place where the decedent intended to live permanently (see the glossary for a definition of domicile).

Tax Computation Section. This section must be filled out in order to determine what the federal tax will be on the estate. Remember that no taxes will be due if the value of the gross estate as of 1987 is less than $600,000. The gross estate is computed by adding the value of all estate assets and subtracting certain allowable deductions. These computations are made in the Recapitulation section on page three of Form 706. The Recapitulation section lists different categories of estate assets, like real estate, stocks, and life insurance. It also asks the executor to attach the appropriate schedule that describes particular assets in more detail. For instance, Schedule A—Real Estate should be used by the executor to list all real estate that is in the decedent's estate. After the value of the real estate is determined, the total from Schedule A should be put on line 1 of the Recapitulation section. The same procedure should be followed for all other assets.

After the gross estate is computed on line 10, the executor is then entitled to take certain deductions from the gross estate on lines 11 through 19 of the Recapitulation section. As is the case with the asset schedules, the executor should use the corresponding schedules to list more detailed information about certain categories of deductions. These deductions include funeral expenses, mortgages on estate property, and the marital deduction. For instance, Schedule M is used to determine what part of property left to the decedent's spouse can be deducted from the gross estate as the marital deduction.

Form **706**
(Rev. March 1985)
Department of the Treasury
Internal Revenue Service

United States Estate Tax Return

Estate of a citizen or resident of the United States (see separate instructions)
To be filed for decedents dying after December 31, 1981, and before January 1, 1988.
Section references are to the Internal Revenue Code.

OMB No. 1545-0015
Expires 12-31-87

Decedent's first name and middle initial (and maiden name, if any)	Decedent's last name		Date of death
Domicile at time of death	Year domicile established	Date of birth	**Decedent's social security no.**

Name of executor (see instructions)	Executor's address (number and street including apartment number or rural route, city, town or post office, state and ZIP code)
Executor's social security number (see instructions)	

Name and location of court where will was probated or estate administered	Case number

If decedent died testate, check here ▶ ☐ and attach a certified copy of the will. | If Form 4768 is attached, check here ▶ ☐

Authorization to receive confidential tax information under regulations section 601.502(c)(3)(ii), to act as the estate's representative before the Internal Revenue Service, and to make written or oral presentations on behalf of the estate if return prepared by an attorney, accountant, or enrolled agent for the executor:

Name of representative (print or type)	State	Address (number and street, city, state and ZIP code)

I declare that I am the attorney/accountant/enrolled agent (strike out the words that do not apply) for the executor and prepared this return for the executor. I am not under suspension or disbarment from practice before the Internal Revenue Service and am qualified to practice in the State shown above—

Signature	Date	Telephone number

Tax Computation

1	Total gross estate (from Recapitulation, page 3, item 10)			1
2	Total allowable deductions (from Recapitulation, page 3, item 20)			2
3	Taxable estate (subtract line 2 from line 1)			3
4	Adjusted taxable gifts (total taxable gifts (within the meaning of section 2503) made by the decedent after December 31, 1976, other than gifts that are includible in decedent's gross estate (section 2001(b)))			4
5	Add line 3 and line 4			5
6	Tentative tax on the amount on line 5 from Table A in the instructions			6
7	Total gift taxes payable with respect to gifts made by the decedent after December 31, 1976. Include gift taxes paid by the decedent's spouse for split gifts (section 2513) only if the decedent was the donor of these gifts and they are includible in the decedent's gross estate			7
8	Gross estate tax (subtract line 7 from line 6)			8
9	Unified credit against estate tax from Table B in the instructions	9		
10	Adjustment to unified credit. See instructions	10		
11	Allowable unified credit (subtract line 10 from line 9)			11
12	Subtract line 11 from line 8 (but do not enter less than zero)			12
13	Credit for State death taxes. Do not enter more than line 12. Compute credit by using amount on line 3 less $60,000. See Table C in the instructions and **attach credit evidence** (see instructions)			13
14	Subtract line 13 from line 12			14
15	Credit for Federal gift taxes on pre-1977 gifts (section 2012) (attach computation)	15		
16	Credit for foreign death taxes (from Schedule(s) P). (Attach Form(s) 706CE)	16		
17	Credit for tax on prior transfers (from Schedule Q)	17		
18	Total (add lines 15, 16, and 17)			18
19	Net estate tax (subtract line 18 from line 14)			19
20	Prior payments. Explain in an attached statement	20		
21	United States Treasury bonds redeemed in payment of estate tax	21		
22	Total (add lines 20 and 21)			22
23	Balance due (subtract line 22 from line 19)			23

Note: *Please attach the necessary supplemental documents.* ***You must attach the Death Certificate.***

Under penalties of perjury, I declare that I have examined this return, including accompanying schedules and statements, and to the best of my knowledge and belief, it is true, correct, and complete. Declaration of preparer other than the executor is based on all information of which preparer has any knowledge.

Signature(s) of executor(s) | Date

Signature of preparer other than executor | Address (and ZIP code) | Date

For Paperwork Reduction Act Notice, see page 1 of the instructions. Form **706** (Rev. 3-85)

Form 706 (Rev. 3-85)

Estate of:

Elections by the Executor

Please check the "Yes" or "No" box for each question.	Yes	No
1 Do you elect alternate valuation?		
2 Do you elect special use valuation? If "Yes," complete and attach Schedule N and the agreements required by the instructions to Schedule N.		
3 Are you excluding from the decedent's gross estate the value of a lump-sum distribution described in section 2039(f)(2)? If "Yes," you must attach the information required by the instructions.		
4 Do you elect to claim a marital deduction for qualified terminable interest property (QTIP) under section 2056(b)(7)? If "Yes," please attach the additional information required by the instructions.		
5 Do you elect to pay the tax in installments as described in section 6166? If "Yes," you must attach the additional information described in the instructions.		
6 Do you elect to postpone the part of the tax attributable to a reversionary or remainder interest as described in section 6163?		
7 Do you elect to have part or all of the estate tax liability assumed by an ESOP as described in section 2210? If "Yes," enter the amount of tax assumed by the ESOP here $ ________ and attach the supplemental statements described in the instructions.		

General Information

1 Death certificate number and issuing authority (attach a copy of the death certificate to this return).

2 Decedent's business or occupation. If retired check here ▶ ☐ and state decedent's former business or occupation.

3 Marital status of the decedent at time of death:

☐ Married

☐ Widow or widower—Name and date of death of deceased spouse ▶ ________

☐ Single

☐ Legally separated

☐ Divorced—Date divorce decree became final

4a Surviving spouse's name	4b Social security number	4c Amount received (see instructions)

5 Individuals (other than the surviving spouse), trusts, or other estates who receive benefits from the estate (do not include charitable beneficiaries shown in Schedule O) (see instructions). For Privacy Act Notice (applicable to individual beneficiaries only), see the Instructions for Form 1040.

Name of individual, trust or estate receiving $5,000 or more	Identifying number	Relationship to decedent	Amount (see instructions)
All unascertainable beneficiaries and those who receive less than $5,000 ▶			
Total			

(Continued on next page)

Page 2

Form 706 (Rev. 3-85)

Estate of:

Please check the "Yes" or "No" box for each question.		Yes	No
6	Does the gross estate contain any section 2044 property (see instructions)?		
7a	Have Federal gift tax returns ever been filed? If "Yes," please attach copies of the returns, if available, and furnish the following information:		
7b	Period(s) covered — 7c Internal Revenue office(s) where filed		
If you answer "Yes" to any of questions 8-16, you must attach additional information as described in the instructions.			
8a	Was there any insurance on the decedent's life that is not included on the return as part of the gross estate?		
8b	Did the decedent own any insurance on the life of another that is not included in the gross estate?		
9	Did the decedent at the time of death own any property as a joint tenant with right of survivorship in which (1) one or more of the other joint tenants was someone other than the decedent's spouse and (2) less than the full value of the property is included on the return as part of the gross estate?		
10	Did the decedent, at the time of death, own any interest in a partnership or unincorporated business or any stock in an inactive or closely held corporation?		
11	Are any of the contents of any safe deposit box which the decedent either owned or had access to not included on the return as part of the gross estate?		
12	Did the decedent make any transfer described in section 2035, 2036, 2037 or 2038 (see the instructions for Schedule G)?		
13	Were there in existence at the time of the decedent's death:		
a	Any trusts created by the decedent during his or her lifetime?		
b	Any trusts not created by the decedent under which the decedent possessed any power, beneficial interest or trusteeship?		
14	Did the decedent ever possess, exercise or release any general power of appointment?		
15	Was the marital deduction computed under the transitional rule of Public Law 97-34, section 403(e)(3) (Economic Recovery Tax Act of 1981)? If "Yes," attach a separate computation of the marital deduction, enter the amount on item 18 of the Recapitulation, and note on item 18 "computation attached."		
16	Was the decedent, immediately before death, receiving an annuity described in the "General" paragraph of the instructions for Schedule I?		

Recapitulation

Item number	Gross estate	Alternate value	Value at date of death
1	Schedule A—Real Estate		
2	Schedule B—Stocks and Bonds		
3	Schedule C—Mortgages, Notes, and Cash		
4	Schedule D—Insurance on the Decedent's Life (attach Form(s) 712)		
5	Schedule E—Jointly Owned Property (attach Form(s) 712 for life insurance)		
6	Schedule F—Other Miscellaneous Property (attach Form(s) 712 for life insurance)		
7	Schedule G—Transfers During Decedent's Life (attach Form(s) 712 for life insurance)		
8	Schedule H—Powers of Appointment		
9	Schedule I—Annuities		
10	Total gross estate (add items 1 through 9). Enter here and on page 1, line 1		

Item number	Deductions	Amount
11	Schedule J—Funeral Expenses and Expenses Incurred in Administering Property Subject to Claims	
12	Schedule K—Debts of the Decedent	
13	Schedule K—Mortgages and Liens	
14	Total of items 11 through 13	
15	Allowable amount of deductions from item 14 (see the instructions for item 15 of the Recapitulation)	
16	Schedule L—Net Losses During Administration	
17	Schedule L—Expenses Incurred in Administering Property Not Subject to Claims	
18	Schedule M—Bequests, etc., to Surviving Spouse	
19	Schedule O—Charitable, Public, and Similar Gifts and Bequests	
20	Total allowable deductions (add items 15 through 19). Enter here and on page 1, line 2	

Page 3

Form 706 (Rev. 3-85)

Estate of:

SCHEDULE A—Real Estate

(For jointly owned property that must be disclosed on Schedule E, see the Instructions for Schedule E.)
(Real estate that is part of a sole proprietorship should be shown on Schedule F.)

Item number	Description	Alternate valuation date	Alternate value	Value at date of death
1				
Total from continuation schedule(s) (or additional sheet(s)) attached to this schedule				
TOTAL. (Also enter on the Recapitulation, page 3, at item 1.)				

(If more space is needed, attach the continuation schedule from the end of this package or additional sheets of the same size.)

Schedule A—Page 4

Form 706 (Rev. 3-85)

Estate of:

SCHEDULE B—Stocks and Bonds

(For jointly owned property that must be disclosed on Schedule E, see the Instructions for Schedule E.)

Item number	Description including face amount of bonds or number of shares and par value where needed for identification. Give CUSIP number if available.	Unit value	Alternate valuation date	Alternate value	Value at date of death
1					
Total from continuation schedules(s) (or additional sheet(s)) attached to this schedule . . .					
TOTAL. (Also enter on the Recapitulation, page 3, at item 2.)					

(If more space is needed, attach the continuation schedule from the end of this package or additional sheets of the same size.)

Schedule B—Page 5

Form 706 (Rev. 3-85)

Estate of:

SCHEDULE C—Mortgages, Notes, and Cash

(For jointly owned property that must be disclosed on Schedule E, see the Instructions for Schedule E.)

Item number	Description	Alternate valuation date	Alternate value	Value at date of death
1				
Total from continuation schedule(s) (or additional sheet(s)) attached to this schedule . . .				
TOTAL. (Also enter on the Recapitulation, page 3, at item 3.)				

(If more space is needed, attach the continuation schedule from the end of this package or additional sheets of the same size.)

Schedule C—Page 6

Form 706 (Rev. 3-85)

Estate of:

SCHEDULE D—Insurance on the Decedent's Life

Item number	Description	Alternate valuation date	Alternate value	Value at date of death
1				
	Total from continuation schedule(s) (or additional sheet(s)) attached to this schedule . . .			
	TOTAL. (Also enter on the Recapitulation, page 3, at item 4.)			

(If more space is needed, attach the continuation schedule from the end of this package or additional sheets of the same size.)

Schedule D—Page 7

Form 706 (Rev. 3-85)

Estate of:

SCHEDULE E—Jointly Owned Property

PART I.— Qualified Joint Interests—Interests Held by the Decedent and His or Her Spouse as the Only Joint Tenants (Section 2040(b)(2))

Item number	Description For securities, give CUSIP number, if available.	Alternate valuation date	Alternate value	Value at date of death
	Total from continuation schedule(s) (or additional sheet(s)) attached to this schedule.			
1(a)	Totals.			
1(b)	Amounts included in gross estate (½ of line 1(a))			

PART II.— All Other Joint Interests

2(a) State the name and address of each surviving co-tenant. If there are more than 3 surviving co-tenants list the additional co-tenants on an attached sheet.

	Name	Address (Number and street, city, State, and ZIP code)
A.		
B.		
C.		

Item number	Enter letter for co-tenant	Description (including alternate valuation date if any) For securities, give CUSIP number, if available.	Percentage includible	Includible alternate value	Includible value at date of death
		Total from continuation schedule(s) (or additional sheet(s)) attached to this schedule			
2(b)		Total other joint interests			
		Total includible joint interests (add lines 1(b) and 2(b)). Also enter on the Recapitulation, page 3, at item 5 .			

(If more space is needed, attach the continuation schedule from the end of this package or additional sheets of the same size.)

Schedule E—Page 8

Form 706 (Rev. 3-85)

Estate of:

SCHEDULE F—Other Miscellaneous Property Not Reportable Under Any Other Schedule

(For jointly owned property that must be disclosed on Schedule E, see the Instructions for Schedule E.)

		Yes	No
1	Did the decedent, at the time of death, own any articles of artistic or collectible value in excess of $3,000 or any collections whose artistic or collectible value combined at date of death exceeded $10,000? . . . . If "Yes," full details must be submitted on this schedule.		
2	Has the decedent's estate, spouse, or any other person, received (or will receive) any bonus or award as a result of the decedent's employment or death?. . . . . If "Yes," full details must be submitted on this schedule.		
3	Did the decedent at the time of death have, or have access to, a safe deposit box?. . . . . If "Yes," state location, and if held in joint names of decedent and another, state name and relationship of joint depositor. If any of the contents of the safe deposit box are omitted from the schedules in this return, explain fully why omitted.		

Item number	Description For securities, give CUSIP number, if available.	Alternate valuation date	Alternate value	Value at date of death
1				
	Total from continuation schedule(s) (or additional sheet(s)) attached to this schedule . . .			
	TOTAL. (Also enter on the Recapitulation, page 3, at item 6.)			

(If more space is needed, attach the continuation schedule from the end of this package or additional sheets of the same size.)

Schedule F—Page 9

Form 706 (Rev. 3-85)

Estate of:

SCHEDULE G—Transfers During Decedent's Life

Item number	Description For securities, give CUSIP number, if available.	Alternate valuation date	Alternate value	Value at date of death
	A. Gift tax paid by the decedent or the estate for all gifts made by the decedent or his or her spouse within 3 years before the decedent's death (section 2035(c))	X X X X X		
1	**B.** Transfers includible under sections 2035(a), 2036, 2037 or 2038:			
Total from continuation schedule(s) (or additional sheet(s)) attached to this schedule				
TOTAL. (Also enter on the Recapitulation, page 3, at item 7.)				

SCHEDULE H—Powers of Appointment

Item number	Description	Alternate valuation date	Alternate value	Value at date of death
1				
Total from continuation schedule(s) (or additional sheet(s)) attached to this schedule . . .				
TOTAL. (Also enter on the Recapitulation, page 3, at item 8.)				

(If more space is needed, attach the continuation schedule from the end of this package or additional sheets of the same size.)

Schedules G and H—Page 10

Form 706 (Rev. 3-85)

Estate of:

SCHEDULE I—Annuities

Note: *The total combined exclusion for lump sum distributions and "Annuities Under Approved Plans" is **$100,000** for the estates of certain decedents dying after December 31, 1982. No exclusion is generally allowed for the estates of decedents dying after December 31, 1984 (see instructions).*

Item number	Description Show the entire value of the annuity before any exclusions.	Alternate valuation date	Includible alternate value	Includible value at date of death
1				
Total from continuation schedule(s) (or additional sheet(s)) attached to this schedule . . .				
TOTAL. (Also enter on the Recapitulation, page 3, at item 9.)				

(If more space is needed, attach the continuation schedule from the end of this package or additional sheets of the same size.)

Schedule I—Page 11

Form 706 (Rev. 3-85)

Estate of:

SCHEDULE J—Funeral Expenses and Expenses Incurred in Administering Property Subject to Claims

Note: *Do not list on this schedule expenses of administering property not subject to claims. For those expenses, see the Instructions for Schedule L.*

If executors' commissions, attorney fees, etc., are claimed and allowed as a deduction for estate tax purposes, they are not allowable as a deduction in computing the taxable income of the estate for Federal income tax purposes. They are allowable as an income tax deduction on Form 1041 if a waiver is filed to waive the deduction on Form 706 (see Form 1041 instructions).

Item number	Description	Expense amount	Total Amount
	A. Funeral expenses:		
1			
	Total funeral expenses		
	B. Administration expenses:		
1	Executors' commissions—amount estimated/agreed upon/paid. (Strike out the words that do not apply.)		
2	Attorney fees—amount estimated/agreed upon/paid. (Strike out the words that do not apply.).		
3	Accountant fees—amount estimated/agreed upon/paid. (Strike out the words that do not apply.).		
		Expense amount	
4	Miscellaneous expenses.		
	Total miscellaneous expenses from continuation schedule(s) (or additional sheet(s)) attached to this schedule		
	Total miscellaneous expenses		
	TOTAL. (Also enter on the Recapitulation, page 3, at item 11.)		

(If more space is needed, attach the continuation schedule from the end of this package or additional sheets of the same size.) **Schedule J—Page 12**

Form 706 (Rev. 3-85)

Estate of:

SCHEDULE K—Debts of the Decedent, and Mortgages and Liens

Item number	Debts of the Decedent—Creditor and nature of claim, and allowable death taxes	Amount
1		
	Total from continuation schedule(s) (or additional sheet(s)) attached to this schedule	
	TOTAL. (Also enter on the Recapitulation, page 3, at item 12.)	

Item number	Mortgages and Liens—Description	Amount
1		
	Total from continuation schedule(s) (or additional sheet(s)) attached to this schedule	
	TOTAL. (Also enter on the Recapitulation, page 3, at item 13.)	

SCHEDULE L—Net Losses During Administration and Expenses Incurred in Administering Property Not Subject to Claims

Item number	Net losses during administration (**Note:** *Do not deduct losses claimed on a Federal income tax return.*)	Amount
1		
	Total from continuation schedule(s) (or additional sheet(s)) attached to this schedule	
	TOTAL. (Also enter on the Recapitulation, page 3, at item 16.)	

Item number	Expenses incurred in administering property not subject to claims (Indicate whether estimated, agreed upon, or paid.)	Amount
1		
	Total from continuation schedule(s) (or additional sheet(s)) attached to this schedule	
	TOTAL. (Also enter on the Recapitulation, page 3, at item 17.)	

(If more space is needed, attach the continuation schedule from the end of this package or additional sheets of the same size.)

Schedules K and L—Page 13

Form 706 (Rev. 3-85)

Estate of:

SCHEDULE M—Bequests, etc., to Surviving Spouse

	Yes	No
1 Did any property pass to the surviving spouse as a result of a qualified disclaimer?. . . . . *If "Yes," attach a copy of the written disclaimer required by section 2518(b).*		

Item number	Description of property interests passing to surviving spouse	Value
1		
	Total from continuation schedule(s) (or additional sheet(s)) attached to this schedule	

2 Total . . . .

3 **(a)** Federal estate tax payable out of property interests listed above . . . .

(b) Other death taxes payable out of property interests listed above . . . .

(c) Add items (a) and (b) . . . .

4 Net value of property interests listed above (subtract 3(c) from 2). Also enter on the Recapitulation, page 3, at item 18. . . .

(If more space is needed, attach the continuation schedule from the end of this package or additional sheets of the same size.)

Schedule M—Page 14

Form 706 (Rev. 3-85)

Estate of:

SCHEDULE N—Section 2032A Valuation

Enter the requested information for each party who received any interest in the specially valued property. **Also complete and attach the required agreements described in the instructions.**

	Name	Address
A		
B		
C		
D		
E		
F		
G		
H		

	Identifying number	Relationship to decedent	Fair market value	Special use value
A				
B				
C				
D				
E				
F				
G				
H				

SCHEDULE O—Charitable, Public, and Similar Gifts and Bequests

		Yes	No
1(a)	If the transfer was made by will, has any action been instituted to have interpreted or to contest the will or any provision thereof affecting the charitable deductions claimed in this schedule?		
	If "Yes," full details must be submitted with this schedule.		
1(b)	According to the information and belief of the person or persons filing the return, is any such action designed or contemplated? . . . If "Yes," full details must be submitted with this schedule.		
2	Did any property pass to charity as the result of a qualified disclaimer? . . . . . If "Yes," attach a copy of the written disclaimer required by section 2518(b).		

Item number	Name and address of beneficiary	Character of institution	Amount
1			
Total from continuation schedule(s) (or additional sheet(s)) attached to this schedule			
3 Total			
4 (a) Federal estate tax payable out of property interests listed above			
(b) Other death taxes payable out of property interests listed above			
(c) Add items (a) and (b)			
5 Net value of property interests listed above (subtract 4(c) from 3). Also enter on the Recapitulation, page 3, at item 19 . . .			

(If more space is needed, attach the continuation schedule from the end of this package or additional sheets of the same size.)

Schedules N and O—Page 15

Form 706 (Rev. 3-85)

Estate of:

SCHEDULE P—Credit for Foreign Death Taxes

List all foreign countries to which death taxes have been paid and for which a credit is claimed on this return.

If a credit is claimed for death taxes paid to more than one foreign country, compute the credit for taxes paid to one country on this sheet and attach a separate copy of Schedule P for each of the other countries.

The credit computed on this sheet is for .... (Name of death tax or taxes)

.... imposed in .... (Name of country)

Credit is computed under the .... (Insert title of treaty or "statute")

Citizenship (Nationality) of decedent at time of death ....

(All amounts and values must be entered in United States money)

1	Total of estate, inheritance, legacy and succession taxes imposed in the country named above attributable to property situated in that country, subjected to these taxes, and included in the gross estate (as defined by statute)	
2	Value of the gross estate (adjusted, if necessary, according to the instructions for item 2)	
3	Value of property situated in that country, subjected to death taxes imposed in that country, and included in the gross estate (adjusted, if necessary, according to the instructions for item 3)	
4	Tax imposed by section 2001 reduced by the total credits claimed under sections 2010, 2011, and 2012 (see instructions)	
5	Amount of Federal estate tax attributable to property specified at item 3. (Divide item 3 by item 2 and multiply the result by item 4.)	
6	Credit for death taxes imposed in the country named above (the smaller of item 1 or item 5). Also enter on page 1, line 16	

SCHEDULE Q—Credit for Tax on Prior Transfers

	Name of transferor	Social security number	IRS office where estate tax return was filed	Date of death
A				
B				
C				

Check here ▶ ☐ if section 2013(f) (special valuation of farm, etc., real property) adjustments to the computation of the credit were made (see instructions).

Check here ▶ ☐ if section 2013(g) (generation-skipping transfers) adjustments to the computation of the credit were made (see instructions).

Item	Transferor A	Transferor B	Transferor C	Total A, B, & C
1 Transferee's tax as apportioned (from worksheet, (line 7 + line 8) x line 35 for each column)				
2 Transferor's tax (from each column of worksheet, line 20)				
3 Maximum amount before percentage requirement (for each column, enter amount from line 1 or 2, whichever is smaller)				
4 Percentage allowed (each column) (see instructions)	%	%	%	
5 Credit allowable (line 3 x line 4 for each column)				
6 TOTAL credit allowable (add columns A, B, and C of line 5). Enter here and on line 17 of the Tax Computation.				

Schedules P and Q—Page 16

Form 706 (Rev. 3-85) (Make copies of this schedule before completing it if you will need more than one schedule)

Estate of:

CONTINUATION SCHEDULE

Continuation of Schedule ______
(Enter letter of schedule you are continuing)

Item number	Description For securities, give CUSIP number, if available.	Unit value (Sch. B only)	Alternate valuation date	Alternate value	Value at date of death or amount deductible
1					
TOTAL. (Carry forward to main schedule)					

See instructions on back.

Continuation Schedule—Page 17

Instructions for Continuation Schedule

The Continuation Schedule on page 17 provides a uniform format for listing additional assets from Schedules A, B, C, D, E, F, G, H, and I and additional deductions from Schedules J, K, L, M, and O. Use the Continuation Schedule when you need to list more assets or deductions than you have room for on one of the main schedules.

Use a separate Continuation Schedule for each main schedule you are continuing. For each schedule of Form 706, you may use as many Continuation Schedules as needed to list all the assets or deductions to be reported. Do not combine assets or deductions from different schedules on one Continuation Schedule. Since there is only one Continuation Schedule in this package, you should make copies of the schedule before completing it if you expect to need more than one.

Enter the letter of the schedule you are continuing in the space provided at the top of the Continuation Schedule. Complete the rest of the Continuation Schedule as explained in the instructions for the schedule you are continuing. Use the Unit Value column only if you are continuing Schedule B. For all other schedules, you may use the space under the Unit Value column to continue your description.

To continue Schedule E, Part II, you should enter the Percentage includible in the Alternate valuation date column of the Continuation Schedule.

To continue Schedules J, K, L, and M, you should use the Alternate valuation date, and Alternate value columns of the Continuation Schedule to continue your description of the deductions. You should enter the amount of each deduction in the Amount deductible column of the Continuation Schedule.

To continue Schedule O, you should use the space under the Alternate valuation date and Alternate value columns of the Continuation Schedule to provide the Character of institution information required on Schedule O. You should enter the amount of each deduction in the Amount deductible column of the Continuation Schedule.

Carry the total from the Continuation Schedule(s) forward to the appropriate line of the main schedule.

☆ U.S. Government Printing Office: 1987—186-983

Appendix B. Sample List of Beneficiaries, Assets, and Liabilities

The following is a form that can be used to make a list of potential will beneficiaries, assets, and liabilities. This form is not exhaustive, but you can use this format to help organize your own thoughts before preparing your will. It should be kept in the same place that you keep your other personal papers. Also, make sure to tell your executor where the form is so that he or she can use it to prepare a preliminary inventory of your estate assets.

1. Name:
   Address:
   Birth date:
   Telephone:
   Social security number:
   2. Names of immediate family:
      Mother:
      Father:
      Brothers:
      Husband:
      Children:
   3. Names of unrelated friends:
   4. Names of attorney and business advisors:
      Attorney/Address:
      Attorney/Phone:

Assets

Personal

	Net Value
1. Checking account number ______, with ______, located at ______, Anywhere, U.S.A.	$
2. Savings account number ______, with ______, located at ______, Anywhere, U.S.A.	$
3. Stocks and bonds: (If you have any, list the name of the broker and any identification numbers.)	$
4. Notes receivable: (List any money that is owed to you and evidenced by a promissory note.)	$
5. Life insurance with a death benefit: insured by ______, located at ______, Anywhere, U.S.A.	$

Real Estate

	Net Value
1. Specify type of building: Address: Co-owner: Phone:	$

Liabilities

	Amount
1. Mortgages: Mortgage holder:	$
2. Charge-card debts: Charge-card company: Address:	$
3. Other:	

Total Assets $
Total Liabilities $
Estate Net Value $

Appendix C. Sample Will for a Single Person

LAST WILL AND TESTAMENT

I, ______, do hereby make and declare this my last will and testament. I also hereby revoke all wills and codicils made by me prior to this. My address is ________________________ *(street number and name/city or town/state)*.

1. I hereby appoint ______, whose address is ________________ *(street number and name/city or town/state)*, to be my executor. If ______ does not survive me or for some other reason is unable or ceases to be my executor, then I appoint ______ to be my executor. I direct my executor to pay all taxes associated with my death, the expenses of the administration of my estate, and all just debts and claims against my estate. I also direct my executor to pay my funeral expenses and to carry out my funeral arrangements as set forth in the second numbered paragraph below.

2. I direct my executor to have my body prepared for burial at ________________ *(name of funeral home/street name and number/city or town/state)*, and buried at ________________ *(name of cemetery/street name and number/city or town/state)*. I have already discussed my funeral arrangements with the director of ____________ *(name of funeral home)* and have filled out an invoice for the desired arrangements. A copy of the unpaid invoice can be found ____________ *(be specific about the location)*. My executor should pay my funeral expenses out of my estate and have a suitable marker erected at my grave. (For appropriate language on cremation, see page 14.)

3. I give and bequeath to ______________ *(name of family member or friend)* my ______________ *(list certain personal property and be as specific as possible, listing serial numbers, if any)*. (Add additional numbered paragraphs to make as many bequests as you like. Remember that a bequest can be a cash gift.)

4. I give and devise to ______________ *(name of family member or friend)* my ______________ *(list certain real estate and be as specific as possible, naming location and deed identification number, if any)*. (Add additional numbered paragraphs to make as many gifts of real estate as you like.)

5. A bequest or devise given in this will to someone who does not survive me shall instead be liquidated by my executor, and the proceeds shall go to ______________ *(name of beneficiary or perhaps favorite charity/street name and number/city or town/state)*.

6. All of the remainder of my property, whether real or personal or of whatever kind or description, to which in any way I shall be entitled, I give, bequeath and devise to ______________ *(name of family member, friend, or perhaps favorite charity)*.

7. I also direct that my executor shall be excused from furnishing bond.

IN TESTIMONY WHEREOF, I SUBSCRIBE MY NAME AND AFFIX MY SEAL, THIS _____ DAY OF _____ IN THE YEAR _____.

_____ _____ (Seal)
(sign here.)

SIGNED, SEALED, AND DECLARED BY THE ABOVE NAMED TESTATOR IN THE PRESENCE OF THE FOLLOWING WITNESSES WHO SUBSCRIBE OUR NAMES AS WITNESSES AT HIS/HER REQUEST AND IN HIS/HER PRESENCE:

Name	Address
1. _____	_____
2. _____	_____
3. _____	_____

Appendix D. Sample Will for a Married Person with Children

LAST WILL AND TESTAMENT

I, ______, do hereby make and declare this my last will and testament. I also hereby revoke all wills and codicils made by me prior to this. My address is ______________________ *(street number and name/city or town/state)*.

1. I hereby appoint my husband (or wife) ______ to be my executor. If he (or she) does not survive me or for some other reason is unable or ceases to be my executor, then I appoint ______ to be my executor. I direct my executor to pay all taxes associated with my death, the expenses of the administration of my estate, and all just debts and claims against my estate. I also direct my executor to pay my funeral expenses and to carry out my funeral arrangements as set forth in the second numbered paragraph below.

2. I direct my executor to have my body prepared for burial at ______________________ *(name of funeral home/street name and number/city or town/state)*, and buried at ______________________ *(name of cemetery/street name and number/city or town/state)*. I have already discussed my funeral arrangements with the director of ____________ *(name of funeral home)* and have filled out an invoice for the desired arrangements. A copy of the unpaid invoice can be found ______________ *(be specific about the location)*. My executor should pay my funeral expenses out of my estate and have a suitable marker erected at my grave. (For appropriate language on cremation, see page 14.)

3. Except for the bequest in favor of my children listed below, I

hereby give, devise, and bequeath to my husband (or wife) all of the rest of my estate, real or personal or of whatever nature.

4. I give and devise to ______ *(name of particular child)* my ______ *(list certain real estate and be as specific as possible, naming location and deed identification number, if any)*. (Add additional numbered paragraphs to make as many devises as you like.)

5. I give and bequeath to ______ *(name of particular child)* my ______ *(list certain personal property and be as specific as possible listing serial numbers, if any)*. (Add additional numbered paragraphs to make as many bequests to your children as you like. Remember that a bequest can include a cash gift.)

6. A bequest or devise given in this will to someone who does not survive me shall instead be liquidated by my executor, and the proceeds shall go to ______ *(name of beneficiary or perhaps favorite charity/street name and number/city or town/state)*.

7. I also direct that my executor shall be excused from furnishing bond.

IN TESTIMONY WHEREOF, I SUBSCRIBE MY NAME AND AFFIX MY SEAL, THIS ______ DAY OF ______ IN THE YEAR ______.

______ ______ (Seal)
(sign here.)

SIGNED, SEALED, AND DECLARED BY THE ABOVE NAMED TESTATOR IN THE PRESENCE OF THE FOLLOWING WITNESSES WHO SUBSCRIBE OUR NAMES AS WITNESSES AT HIS/HER REQUEST AND IN HIS/HER PRESENCE:

Name	Address
1.______	______
2.______	______
3.______	______

Appendix E. Sample Codicil

I, ______, do hereby declare this document to be a codicil to my last will and testament dated the ______ day of ______, 19____. My address is ____________________.
(street name and number/city or town/state)

Whereas, in the named will I gave and devised:

1. ____________________ *(List specific real estate gifts here)* to ____________________ *(name of original beneficiary)*, I now hereby give and devise said gift to ________________ *(name of new beneficiary)*; and

2. ______ to ______, I now hereby give and devise said gift to ______.

Whereas, in the named will I also gave and bequeathed:

1. ____________________ *(List specific personal property gifts here)* to ____________________ *(name of original beneficiary)*, I now hereby give and bequeath said gift to ________________ *(name of new beneficiary)*; and

2. ______ to ______, I now hereby give and bequeath said gift to ______.

In all other respects I hereby confirm and ratify my said will. IN TESTIMONY WHEREOF, I SUBSCRIBE MY NAME AND AFFIX MY SEAL.

THIS ______ DAY OF ______ IN THE YEAR ______.

THE ABOVE DOCUMENT, WHICH CONSISTS OF TWO PAGES, WAS SIGNED, SEALED, AND DECLARED TO US BY THE ABOVE NAMED TESTATOR TO BE A CODICIL TO HIS/HER LAST WILL AND TESTAMENT. THEREAFTER, AT THE REQUEST OF

THE TESTATOR, WE, THE UNDERSIGNED WITNESSES, SIGNED OUR NAMES BELOW AND IN HIS/HER PRESENCE, AND IN THE PRESENCE OF ONE ANOTHER.

Name	Address
1. ______	______
2. ______	______
3. ______	______

Index